EMPLOYMENT PRACTICES SERIES

The Employer's Guide to

C.O.B.R.A.

Self-Administration

www.cobralawguide.com

EMPLOYMENT PRACTICES SERIES

The Employer's Guide to

C.O.B.R.A.

Self-Administration

Diane M. Pfadenhauer, SPHR, Esq.

DataMotion Publishing

New York

The Employer's Guide to C.O.B.R.A. Self-Administration

Library of Congress Control Number: 2010922648

ISBN: 978-0-9815831-2-9

DataMotion Publishing, LLC

1019 Fort Salonga Road, Suite 10-333

Northport, NY 11768-2209

www.datamotionpublishing.com

This book is dedicated to my fellow volunteer members of the Legal and Legislative Committee of the Human Resources Association of New York (HR/NY), the Society of Human Resource Management's largest "100%" chapter, who give tirelessly of themselves in order to educate the 2,000 human resources practitioner members of the association.

Table of Contents

About the Author

Diane M. Pfadenhauer, SPHR, Esq.

With over 20 years of experience in human resources and as an attorney, Diane is president of Employment Practices Advisors, Inc. (www.epadvisorsinc.com), a boutique firm specializing in employment litigation consulting (including workplace investigations and expert witness testimony on human resource practices) and human resource consulting, encompassing a broad spectrum of tactical and strategic human resource practices and compliance including interim staff, risk prevention and developing human resource strategies to support business goals and objectives. She is also a professor in the M.B.A. program at St. Joseph's College in New York. Prior to her position at St. Joseph's, she spent over a decade as an adjunct professor in graduate programs throughout the New York metropolitan area.

An active member in community and professional organizations, Diane is admitted to New York State Bar. As a member of the National Speaker's Association, she is a frequent speaker and writer and her articles have appeared in industry publications including *HR Magazine, HR Advisor, the Journal of Private Equity, Law Technology News, the Journal of Corpo-*

rate Renewal, and periodicals published by Dow Jones, Inc. and the New York State Bar Association. She is certified as a Senior Professional in Human Resources (SPHR) by the Human Resources Certification Institute.

Diane is also the writer of the award winning weblog, *www.strategichrlawyer.com*, read by over 25,000 unique visitors per month from over 50 countries. She was recently awarded the *New York State Liberty Award* for her Pro Bono work in Louisiana following the devastation of Hurricane Katrina.

Diane received her law degree, *cum laude,* from St. John's University School of Law where she was awarded the ABA/BNA Award for Excellence in the Study of Labor and Employment Law. She is a graduate of New York Institute of Technology's Center for Labor and Industrial Relations where she received her M.S., with *distinction.* She received her B.A. from S.U.N.Y. Potsdam, majoring in Industrial Labor Relations.

About Paylogix

In response to a changing benefits environment and employee needs, employers are seeking more choice, greater flexibility and increased value in their employee benefit offerings. To accomplish this, the employer is often tasked with a greater variety of insurers and products in the workplace which leads to increased complexity in benefits management and billing administration. The result can lead to client challenges and lower persistence in product enrollment.

Paylogix is a nationwide Third Party Administrator (TPA) keenly focused on moving data and money related to health and welfare programs at the workplace. In essence, we're in the business of simplifying the business of workplace benefits administration. Our services mitigate the headaches associated with the billing and administration of benefits especially when faced with multiple employee benefit products from multiple insurers. Paylogix processes include managing the eligibility, billing, payroll deduction, premium collection, and premium remittance to the insurers. Paylogix' systems also perform the ongoing reconciliation between the groups and the insurers as well as a number of compliance related tasks, like COBRA administration and discrimination testing, all designed to free the employer from regulatory and administrative hassles.

Paylogix services include Consolidated Billing®, Common Remitter®, Single Point Billing®, single slot and COBRA administration. Regardless of what you call it, the benefits can lead to increased sales and reduced headaches. By partnering with Paylogix, benefits brokers can increase revenue and sell more products within an existing client account. Products may be from virtually any carrier and product additions are made more easily without having to worry about how it might affect payroll deduction administration for your clients.

Paylogix® enables benefit providers, brokers and employers to save time and money while maintaining greater control over the quality of their workplace benefits administration. Many companies take steps to reduce their benefits costs but overlook the resources expended in maintenance, administration and protocol support. Our products and services are the catalysts often used in the delivery of superior employee benefit programs to the advantage of all the members of the employee benefits supply chain. Some of the world's largest insurance organizations and employers use our solutions for their projects to dramatically and quantifiably improve their offering.

www.paylogix.com

Warning–Disclaimer

While this book strives to provide the reader with practical guidance and to provide general education on the topic at hand, it is not a substitute for adequate legal or other professional advice. The opinions within represent the opinions of the authors and editors only and, therefore, should not be construed as a position on the part of any particular organization or entity.

Further, nothing herein should be construed as the rendering of legal or other professional advice and the reader is advised to consult with appropriate counsel for obtaining any advice. By reading this publication, no attorney client relationship exists between the reader and either the author or publisher.

Introduction

The majority of Americans obtain health insurance coverage through their employers and health insurance is one of the most important benefits that employers can provide for their employees. Because of the employer-based health insurance program in existence, the loss of coverage as the result of a loss of eligible employment status has a profound impact on an individual's or families' ability to remain insured. Therefore, in 1985, the Employee Retirement Income Security Act (ERISA) was amended by the Consolidated Omnibus Budget Reconciliation Act (COBRA) to provide the opportunity for employees and other qualified individuals who lost employer based health insurance to continue their coverage as members of the employer's plan.

The early days of COBRA administration were relatively simple. Employers simply sent home-crafted letters to employees and collected checks to apply to insurance premiums. It was not uncommon for individual coverage to cost under $100 per month and family coverage to cost less than $300 per month.

COBRA generally requires group health plans to offer continuation coverage to covered employees, former employees, spouses, former spouses, and dependent children when group health coverage would otherwise be lost due to certain specific events. This coverage is referred to as "continuation coverage" and for the plan participants the coverage generally is the same as what they had when the employee was an active participant on the plan.

COBRA rights are triggered upon the occurrence of a "qualifying event." Those events include the death of a covered employee, termination or reduction in the hours of a covered employee's employment for reasons other than gross misconduct, a covered employee's becoming entitled to Medicare, divorce or legal separation of a covered employee and spouse, and a child's loss of dependent status (and therefore coverage) under the plan. Persons eligible for COBRA are referred to as "qualified beneficiaries." COBRA sets rules for how and when continuation coverage must be offered and provided, what specific notices are required and how employees and their families may elect continuation coverage, and what circumstances justify terminating continuation coverage.

Employers generally require individuals to pay for COBRA continuation coverage. The premium that is charged cannot exceed the full cost of the coverage (typically the monthly premium), plus a 2 percent administration charge.

Fast forward to 2010 and COBRA has become one of the most technically complex statutes in the employment arena. Yet, despite this complexity and potential for significant liability for employers, all too often employers attempt to navigate the waters of COBRA administration alone. While it is somewhat comical that many refer to the law as the "Continuation of Benefits Act" and laud it for its ability to quickly induce sleep, the truth is that most employers fail to comply with even some of its most basic requirements. Moreover, many employers are unwilling to expend the minimal amount that outsourced professionals might charge to administer COBRA for them. In addition, sadly, many of these supposed outside experts themselves administer COBRA incorrectly.

To add to the complexity, COBRA continuation coverage laws are administered by several federal and state agencies. The Departments of Labor and the Treasury have jurisdiction over private-sector group health plans. The Department of Health and Human Services administers the continuation coverage law as it affects state and local government health plans. Lastly, many states now have enacted mini-state COBRA laws which mirror the federal law and some even provide greater protection.

The purpose of this book is to provide a basic overview and guide for those who dare to go it alone. It is not intended to be a substitute for legal advice, but rather an overview of the basic requirements for those who are brave enough to administer COBRA on their own.

The information in this book was derived from publicly available sources on COBRA and related legislation and compiled by the author in what is intended to be a usable format. Throughout the book examples from relevant Department of Labor, ERISA, IRS or other regulatory sources have been summarized throughout the text.

The author has also made available on the book's website sample forms in Microsoft Word format which can be downloaded and customized for the user's personal use.

These forms are available at www.cobralawguide.com

1

COBRA's Basic Requirements

Basic Coverage

The plan sponsor of each group health plan must generally permit a "qualified beneficiary" who would otherwise lose coverage as the result of a "qualifying event" to elect to continue the same coverage he/she had under the plan, within a specific election period. The coverage, often referred to as "continuation coverage," may not be conditioned on the basis of insurability.

Group Health Plans Subject to COBRA

COBRA generally applies to all private-sector group health plans maintained by employers that have at least 20 employees (whether full or part time). While this may appear at first to be a simple determination, remember that this is COBRA. The 20 employee threshold is determined by looking at whether the employer has more than 20 employees on more than 50 percent of its typical business days in the previous calendar year. Each part-time employee counts as a fraction of a full-time employee, with the fraction equal to the number of hours that the part-time employee worked divided by the hours an employee must work to be considered full time.

COBRA also applies to plans sponsored by state and local governments. It does not, however, apply to plans sponsored by the federal government or by churches and certain church-related organizations.

When determining whether a plan itself is subject to COBRA's requirements, the plan must first be considered a "group health plan." That means any arrangement that an employer establishes or maintains to provide employees or their families with medical care, whether it is provided through insurance, by a health maintenance organization, out of the employer's assets, or through any other means. Medical care includes, for this purpose, inpatient and outpatient hospital care, physician care, surgery and other major medical benefits, prescription drugs, and dental and vision care. In addition, a group health plan is one that is maintained by an employer or employee organization even if the employer or employee organization does not contribute to it if coverage under the plan would not be available at the same cost to an individual but for the individual's employment-related connection to the employer or employee organization. COBRA does not cover life insurance plans, disability plans or long term care plans.

Further discussion regarding what constitutes a health plan includes the following concepts. If an employer or employee organization maintains a program that furthers general good health, but the program does not relate to the relief or alleviation of health or medical problems and is generally accessible to and used by employees without regard to their physical condition or state of health, that program is not considered a program that provides health care and so is not a group health plan. For example, if an employer maintains a spa, swimming pool, gymnasium, or other exercise/fitness program or facility that is normally accessible to and used by employees for reasons other than relief of health or medical problems, such a facility does not constitute a program that provides health care and thus is not a group health plan. In contrast, if an employer maintains a drug or alcohol treatment program or a health clinic, or any other facility or program that is intended to relieve or alleviate a physical condition or health problem, the facility or program is considered to be the provision of health care and so is considered a group health plan.

Small Employer Plans

Since many states have enacted mini-COBRA laws that mirror the federal COBRA law, the issue of continuation coverage can sometimes be blurred. The federal COBRA law has very specific guidance regarding what constitutes a small employer plan. Small employer plans are not covered by the federal COBRA law but are increasingly covered by state law. The 20 person threshold described above is the most basic of requirements. As described above, a *small-employer plan* is a group health plan maintained by an employer that normally employed fewer than 20 employees during the preceding calendar year. In the case of a multiemployer plan, a *small-employer plan* is a group health plan under which each of the employers contributing to the plan for a calendar year normally employed fewer than 20 employees during the preceding calendar year.

With respect to a controlled group of corporations, foreign corporations are not excluded from membership in a controlled group of corporations. Thus, a company in the United States with a subsidiary company abroad would include those subsidiary employees in determining whether the federal COBRA law applies.

With respect to determining which employees to include in the calculation, in addition to that described above, the following individuals are not counted as employees for purposes of COBRA: self-employed individuals, independent contractors (and their employees and independent contractors), and directors (in the case of a corporation).

Just when the reader thought the calculation of the 20 employee threshold was already confusing, CO-BRA adds yet more complexity. An employer may determine the number of its employees on a daily basis or a pay period basis. The basis used by the employer must be used with respect to all employees of the employer and must be used for the entire year for which the number of employees is being determined. If an employer determines the number of its employees on a daily basis, it must determine the actual number of full-time employees on each typical business day and the actual number of part-time employees and the hours worked by each of those part-time employees on each typical business day. Each full-time employee counts as one employee on each typical business day and each part-time employee counts as a fraction, with the numerator of the fraction equal to the number of hours worked by that employee and the denominator equal to the number of hours that must be worked on a typical business day in order to be considered a full-time employee. If an employer determines the number of its employees on a pay period basis, it must determine the actual number of full-time employees employed during that pay period and the actual number of part-time employees employed and the hours worked by each of those part-time employees during the pay period. For each day of that pay period, each full-time employee counts as one employee and each part-time employee counts as a fraction, with the numerator of the fraction equal to the number of hours worked by that employee during that pay period and the denominator equal to the number of hours that must be worked during that pay period in order to be considered a full-time employee. The determination of the number of hours required to be considered a full-time employee is based upon the employer's employment practices, except that in no event may the hours required to be considered a full-time employee exceed eight hours for any day or 40 hours for any week.

For multiemployer plans, the determination of whether the plan is a small-employer plan on any particular date depends on which employers are contributing to the plan on that date and on the workforce of those employers during the preceding calendar year. If a plan that is otherwise subject to CO-BRA ceases to be a small-employer plan because of the addition during a calendar year of an employer that did not normally employ fewer than 20 employees on a typical business day during the preceding calendar year, the plan ceases to be excepted from COBRA immediately upon the addition of the new employer. In contrast, if the plan ceases to be a small-employer plan by reason of an increase during a calendar year in the workforce of an employer contributing to the plan, the plan ceases to be excepted from COBRA on the January 1 immediately following the calendar year in which the employer's workforce increased.

So, now what happens if a plan becomes a small employer plan? The following rule applies: if a plan that has been subject to COBRA (that is, was not a small-employer plan) becomes a small-employer plan, the plan remains subject to COBRA for qualifying events that occurred during the period when the plan was subject to COBRA. This is an important consideration for an employer in the current economic climate when trying to ascertain which law applies – federal or, in certain instances, state law. The IRS regulations provide the following example to illustrate this point:

> *An employer maintains a group health plan. The employer employed 20 employees on more than 50 percent of its working days during 2001, and consequently the plan is not excepted from COBRA during 2002. Employee E resigns and does not work for the employer after January 31, 2002. Under the terms of the plan, E is no longer eligible for coverage upon the effective date of the resignation, that is, February 1, 2002. The employer does not hire a replacement for E. E timely elects and pays for COBRA continuation coverage. The employer employs 19 employees for the remainder of 2002, and consequently the plan is not subject to COBRA in 2003. The plan must nevertheless continue to make COBRA continuation coverage available to E during 2003 until the obligation to make COBRA continuation coverage available ceases under the rules of §54.4980B–7. The obligation could continue until August 1, 2003, the date that is 18 months after the date of E's qualifying event, or longer if E is eligible for a disability extension.*

The previous example becomes more confusing when questions concerning eligible dependents come into play:

> *The employer above continues to employ 19 employees throughout 2003 and 2004 and consequently the plan continues to be excepted from COBRA during 2004 and 2005. Spouse S is covered under the plan because S is married to one of the employer's employees. On April 1, 2002, S is divorced from that employee and ceases to be eligible for coverage under the plan. The plan is subject to COBRA during 2002 because X normally employed 20 employees during 2001. S timely notifies the plan administrator of the divorce and timely elects and pays for COBRA continuation coverage. Even though the plan is generally excepted from COBRA during 2003, 2004, and 2005, it must nevertheless continue to make COBRA continuation coverage available to S during those years until the obligation to make COBRA continuation coverage available ceases under the rules of §54.4980B–7. The obligation could continue until April 1, 2005, the date that is 36 months after the date of S's qualifying event.*

Thus, employers must be careful not to terminate the COBRA rights of individuals even though they have dropped under the minimum employee threshold.

COBRA and Cafeteria Plans

The provision of health care benefits does not fail to be a group health plan merely because those benefits are offered under a cafeteria plan (as defined in section 125 of the Internal Revenue Code) or under any other arrangement under which an employee is offered a choice between health care benefits and other taxable or nontaxable benefits. However, the COBRA continuation coverage requirements apply only to the type and level of coverage under the cafeteria plan or other flexible benefit arrangement that a qualified beneficiary is actually receiving on the day before the qualifying event.

Responsibility for Administration of COBRA

Group health plans covered by COBRA that are sponsored by private-sector employers are generally considered welfare plans under ERISA and therefore subject to ERISA's other technical requirements. One such requirement is that group health plans must be administered by someone called a "plan administrator." The plan administrator is generally named in the plan documents. Many group health plans are administered by the employer that sponsors the plan, but some group health plans are administered, in whole or in part, by another individual or organization separate from the employer, such as a professional benefits administration firm. In that case, the professional benefits administration firm may be the plan administrator. Carrying out the requirements of COBRA is the direct responsibility of the plan administrator.

Employers should note, however, that more and more states have enacted mini COBRA laws which mirror the federal COBRA law in their protections. These mini COBRA laws, in many states are at times providing even greater benefits to participants.

Under COBRA's requirements, the right to COBRA continuation coverage and obligations for health plans stem from whether an entity that has the health plan meets the definition of employer.

Generally an employer is a person for whom services are performed. An employer is a successor employer if it results from a consolidation, merger, or similar restructuring of the employer or if it is a mere continuation of the employer.

Multiemployer plans are also subject to COBRA. A multiemployer plan is a plan to which more than one employer is required to contribute, that is maintained pursuant to one or more collective bargaining agreements between one or more employee organizations and more than one employer, and that satisfies such other requirements as the Secretary of Labor may prescribe by regulation.

Type of Benefits Available Under COBRA

The coverage must consist of coverage which, as of the time the coverage is being provided, is identical to the coverage provided under the plan to similarly situated beneficiaries under the plan with respect to whom a qualifying event has not occurred. If coverage is modified under the plan for any group of similarly situated beneficiaries, such coverage is also to be modified in the same manner for all individuals who are qualified beneficiaries under the plan. Thus, the person who elects and continues coverage keeps the identical plan s/he had prior to the qualifying event. If the plan is subsequently modified for active participants, it is also similarly modified for COBRA participants.

If a qualified beneficiary participates in a region-specific benefit package (such as an HMO or an on-site clinic) that will not service her or his health needs in the area to which she or he is relocating (regardless of the reason for the relocation), the qualified beneficiary must be given, within a reasonable period after requesting other coverage, an opportunity to elect alternative coverage that the employer or employee organization makes available to active employees. If the employer or employee organization makes group health plan coverage available to similarly situated nonCOBRA beneficiaries that can be extended in the area to which the qualified beneficiary is relocating, then that coverage is the alternative coverage that must be made available to the relocating qualified beneficiary. If the employer or employee organization does not make group health plan coverage available to similarly situated nonCOBRA beneficiaries that can be extended in the area to which the qualified beneficiary is relocating but makes coverage available to other employees that can be extended in that area, then the coverage made available to those other employees must be made available to the relocating qualified beneficiary. The effective date of the alternative coverage must be no later than the date of the qualified beneficiary's relocation, or, if later, the first day of the month following the month in which the qualified beneficiary requests the alternative coverage. However, the employer or employee organization is not required to make any other coverage available to the relocating qualified beneficiary if the only coverage the employer or employee organization makes available to active employees is not available in the area to which the qualified beneficiary relocates (because all such coverage is region-specific and does not service individuals in that area).

If an employer or employee organization makes an open enrollment period available to similarly situated active employees with respect to whom a qualifying event has not occurred, the same open enrollment period rights must be made available to each qualified beneficiary receiving COBRA continuation coverage. An open enrollment period means a period during which an employee covered under a plan can choose to be covered under another group health plan or under another benefit package within the same plan, or to add or eliminate coverage of family members.

Penalties for Failure to Comply

If a plan does not comply with the COBRA continuation coverage requirements, the Internal Revenue Code imposes an excise tax (currently $110 per day) on the employer maintaining the plan (or on the plan itself), whereas ERISA gives certain parties—including qualified beneficiaries who are participants or beneficiaries within the meaning of Title I of ERISA, as well as the Department of Labor—the right to file a lawsuit to redress the noncompliance.

Generally the excise tax is imposed on the employer maintaining the plan, except that in the case of a multiemployer plan the excise tax is imposed on the plan. In certain other instances, however, the excise tax may also be imposed on a person involved with the provision of benefits under the plan (other than in the capacity of an employee), such as an insurer providing benefits under the plan or a third party administrator administering claims under the plan. In general, such a person will be liable for the excise tax if the person assumes, under a legally enforceable written agreement, the responsibility for performing the act to which the failure to comply with the COBRA continuation coverage requirements relates.

Alternatives to COBRA Continuation Coverage

Those entitled to elect COBRA continuation coverage may have alternative options to COBRA coverage. One option may be "special enrollment" into other group health coverage. Under the Health Insurance Portability and Accountability Act (HIPAA), upon certain events, group health plan and health insurance issuers are required to provide a special enrollment period during which individuals who previously declined coverage for themselves and their dependents, and who are otherwise eligible, may be allowed to enroll without having to wait until the next open season for enrollment. One event that triggers special enrollment is an employee or dependent of an employee losing eligibility for other health coverage. For example, an employee who loses group health coverage may be able to special enroll in a spouse's health plan. The employee or dependent must request special enrollment within 30 days of the loss of other coverage.

If an employee or dependent chooses to elect COBRA instead of special enrollment upon a loss of group health coverage, the employee or dependent will have another opportunity to request special enrollment once COBRA has been exhausted. In order to exhaust COBRA coverage, the individual must receive the maximum period of COBRA coverage available without early termination. To special enroll after exhausting COBRA, an individual must request enrollment within 30 days of the loss of COBRA coverage.

Who Is Entitled to Continuation Coverage?

Again, group health plan is required to offer COBRA continuation coverage only to **qualified beneficiaries** and only after a **qualifying event** has occurred.

Qualified Beneficiaries

A qualified beneficiary is an individual who was covered by a group health plan on the day before a qualifying event occurred and who is an employee, the employee's spouse or former spouse, or the employee's dependent child. In certain cases involving the bankruptcy of the employer, a retired employee, the retired employee's spouse (or former spouse), and the retired employee's dependent children may be qualified beneficiaries. In addition, any child born to or placed for adoption with a covered employee during a period of continuation coverage (that is after COBRA has been elected) is automatically considered a qualified beneficiary. Agents, independent contractors, and directors who participate in the group health plan may also be qualified beneficiaries.

There is a special rule with respect to retirees and widows and widowers. The term qualified beneficiary includes a covered employee who had retired on or before the date of substantial elimination of coverage and any other individual who, on the day before the qualifying event, is a beneficiary under the plan as the spouse of the covered employee, as the dependent child of the employee, or as the surviving spouse of the covered employee.

With respect to the bankruptcy of the employer, a covered employee who had retired on or before the date of substantial elimination of group health plan coverage is also a qualified beneficiary, as is any spouse, surviving spouse, or dependent child of the covered employee if, on the day before the bankruptcy qualifying event, the spouse, surviving spouse, or dependent child is a beneficiary under the plan.

COBRA again rears its ugly head when a discussion of additional or new family members comes into play. While it is common knowledge that the dependents described above may be qualified beneficiaries, the following examples demonstrate that not all new family members and coverage additions or terminations are considered qualified beneficiaries or qualifying events. The IRS regulations demonstrate these exceedingly complex rules with the following examples:

Example 1. (i) B is a single employee who voluntarily terminates employment and elects COBRA continuation coverage under a group health plan. To comply with the requirements of section 9801(f), the plan permits a covered employee who marries to have her or his spouse covered under the plan. One month after electing COBRA continuation coverage, B marries and chooses to have B's spouse covered under the plan.

(ii) B's spouse is not a qualified beneficiary. Thus, if B dies during the period of COBRA continuation coverage, the plan does not have to offer B's surviving spouse an opportunity to elect COBRA continuation coverage.

Example 2. (i) C is a married employee who terminates employment. C elects COBRA continuation coverage for C but not C's spouse, and C's spouse declines to elect such coverage. C's spouse thus ceases to be a qualified beneficiary. At the next open enrollment period, C adds the spouse as a beneficiary under the plan.

(ii) The addition of the spouse during the open enrollment period does not make the spouse a qualified beneficiary. The plan thus will not have to offer the spouse an opportunity to elect COBRA continuation coverage upon a later divorce from or death of C.

Example 3. (i) Under the terms of a group health plan, a covered employee's child, upon attaining age 19, ceases to be a dependent eligible for coverage.

(ii) At that time, the child must be offered an opportunity to elect COBRA continuation coverage. If the child elects COBRA continuation coverage, the child marries during the period of the COBRA continuation coverage, and the child's spouse becomes covered under the group health plan, the child's spouse is not a qualified beneficiary.

Example 4. (i) D is a single employee who, upon retirement, is given the opportunity to elect COBRA continuation coverage but declines it in favor of an alternative offer of 12 months of employer-paid retiree health benefits. At the end of the election period, D ceases to be a qualified beneficiary and will not have to be given another opportunity to elect COBRA continuation coverage (at the end of those 12 months or at any other time). D marries E during the period of retiree health coverage and, under the terms of that coverage, E becomes covered under the plan.

(ii) If a divorce from or death of D will result in E's losing coverage, E will be a qualified beneficiary because E's coverage under the plan on the day before the qualifying event (that is, the divorce or death) will have been by reason of D's acceptance of 12 months of employer-paid coverage after the prior qualifying event (D's retirement) rather than by reason of an election of COBRA continuation coverage.

> *Example 5. (i) The facts are the same as in Example 4, except that, under the terms of the plan, the divorce or death does not cause E to lose coverage so that E continues to be covered for the balance of the original 12-month period.*
>
> *(ii) E does not have to be allowed to elect COBRA continuation coverage because the loss of coverage at the end of the 12-month period is not caused by the divorce or death, and thus the divorce or death does not constitute a qualifying event.*

Qualifying Events

A qualifying event is the occurrence of an event that would otherwise result in the covered employee or his dependent losing coverage. It includes specifically:

1. For the spouse of dependent child, the death of the covered employee.

2. For the employee, spouse or dependent child, the termination (other than by reason of the employee's gross misconduct), or reduction of hours, of the covered employee's employment.

3. For the spouse or dependent child, the divorce or legal separation of the covered employee from the employee's spouse.

4. For the spouse or dependent child, the covered employee becoming entitled to Medicare benefits under title XVIII of the Social Security Act.

5. For the dependent child, his ceasing to be a dependent child under the generally applicable requirements of the plan.

6. A proceeding in bankruptcy under Title 11 of the United States Code with respect to an employer from whose employment a covered employee retired at any time.

In the case of small-employer plans, if the plan later becomes subject to COBRA, it is not required to make COBRA continuation coverage available to anyone whose coverage ends as a result of an event during a year in which the plan is excepted from COBRA. For example, if a group health plan is excepted from CO-BRA as a small-employer plan during the year 2009 and an employee terminates employment on December 31, 2009, the termination is not a qualifying event and the plan is not required to permit the employee to elect COBRA continuation coverage.

A reduction of hours of a covered employee's employment occurs whenever there is a decrease in the hours that a covered employee is required to work or actually works, but only if the decrease is not accompanied by an immediate termination of employment. This is true regardless of whether the covered employee continues to perform services following the reduction of hours of employment. For example, an absence from work due to disability, a temporary layoff, or any other reason (other than due to leave that is FMLA leave described below) is a reduction of hours of a covered employee's employment if there is not an immediate termination of employment. If a group health plan measures eligibility for the coverage of employees by the number of hours worked in a given time period, such as the preceding month or quarter, and an employee covered under the plan fails to work the minimum number of hours during that time period, the failure to work the minimum number of required hours is a reduction of hours of that covered employee's employment.

COBRA contains a provision that an individual who loses coverage as the result of a termination of employment can be denied COBRA coverage if the employment loss was due to gross misconduct. The term "gross misconduct" is not specifically defined in CO-BRA or in regulations under COBRA. Therefore, whether a terminated employee has engaged in gross misconduct that will justify a plan in not offering COBRA to that former employee and his or her family members will depend on the specific facts and circumstances. Generally, it can be assumed that being fired for most ordinary reasons, such as excessive absences or generally poor performance, does not amount to gross misconduct.

The qualifying event of a qualified beneficiary who is a child born to or placed for adoption with a covered employee during a period of COBRA continuation coverage, is the qualifying event giving rise to the period of COBRA continuation coverage during which the child is born or placed for adoption. If a second qualifying event has occurred before the child is born or placed for adoption (such as the death of the covered employee), then the second qualifying event also applies to the newborn or adopted child.

Special Enrollment Rights

Employees eligible to participate in a group health plan (whether or not participating), as well as former employees participating in a plan (referred to as participants), are entitled to special enrollment rights for certain family members upon the loss of other group health plan coverage or upon the acquisition by the employee or participant of a new spouse or of a new dependent through birth, adoption, or placement for adoption, if certain requirements are satisfied. Employees not participating in the plan also can obtain rights for self-enrollment under those rules. Once a qualified beneficiary is receiving COBRA continuation coverage (that is, has timely elected and made timely payment for COBRA continuation coverage), the qualified beneficiary has the same right to enroll family members under those special enrollment rules as if the qualified beneficiary were an employee or participant within the meaning of those rules. However, neither a qualified beneficiary who is not receiving COBRA continuation coverage nor a former qualified beneficiary has any special enrollment rights under those rules.

If the plan covering the qualified beneficiary provides that new family members of active employees can become covered (either automatically or upon an appropriate election) before the next open enrollment period, then the same right must be extended to the new family members of a qualified beneficiary.

If the addition of a new family member will result in a higher applicable premium (for example, if the qualified beneficiary was previously receiving CO-

BRA continuation coverage as an individual, or if the applicable premium for family coverage depends on family size), the plan can require the payment of a correspondingly higher amount for the COBRA continuation coverage.

2

COBRA's Extensive
Notice Requirements

In 2004, COBRA's long awaited regulations governing notices were issued. The regulations increased the complexity of COBRA administration, but at the same time clarified a number of issues with regard to accountability and responsibility for various elements of administration.

Under COBRA, group health plans are required to provide covered employees and their families with specific notices explaining their COBRA rights. Health plans must also have rules for how COBRA continuation coverage is offered, how qualified beneficiaries may elect continuation coverage, and when it can be terminated. All too often, however, those who wish to administer COBRA fail to explore these minute details. It is not at all uncommon for some to pull down sample notices from the web, without any thought to the many decisions which must be made regarding administration.

The Summary Plan Description

The COBRA rights provided under the plan, like other important plan information, must be described in the plan's Summary Plan Description (SPD). The SPD is a written document that gives important information about the plan, including what benefits are available under the plan, the rights of participants and beneficiaries under the plan, and how the plan works. Under ERISA, each plan is required to provide plan participants with the SPD within 90 days after he or she first becomes a participant in a plan (or within 120 days after the plan is first subject to the reporting and disclosure provisions of ERISA).

If there are material changes to the plan, the plan must give participants a Summary of Material Modifications (SMM) not later than 210 days after the end of the plan year in which the changes become effective. If the change is a material reduction in covered services or benefits, the SMM must be furnished not later than 60 days after the reduction is adopted. A participant or beneficiary covered under the plan may request a copy of the SPD and any SMMs (as well as any other plan documents), which must be provided within 30 days of a written request.

Understanding these requirements and putting them into action are, unfortunately, two different things entirely. Many employer administrators mistakenly believe that a short summary provided by the health insurance provider is sufficient notice for plan participants. Unfortunately, this is not sufficient to satisfy either COBRA's or ERISA's requirements. Employers should be sure to obtain the SPD from the insurer and develop a system to provide it to plan participants.

The COBRA General Notice

The first notice that COBRA requires is the general notice. The general notice gives each employee, spouse and dependent children of the employee a summary of COBRA rights. Employees of the employer are deemed to have received the notice if the employer can document that the employee and his/her spouse were provided with the document.

The general notice must be provided within the first 90 days of coverage. Group health plans can satisfy this requirement by including the general notice in the plan's SPD and giving the SPD to the employee and to the spouse within this time limit. Unfortunately, however, employers who choose this method must be sure that the SPD is also given to the employee's spouse. If it is not given to the employee's spouse, then COBRA's requirements are not satisfied. The easiest way to satisfy this requirement is to mail the general notice home to the attention of the employee and spouse.

Part of the reason that COBRA's notice requirements are so complex is that they are not at all boiler plate. As one can immediately see, the notice must be tailored specifically to follow the procedures adopted by the employer or the plan. All too often, employer administrators select the notice and forget about the process.

The general notice must include:

- The name of the plan and the name, address, and telephone number of someone whom the employee and spouse can contact for more information on COBRA and the plan;
- A general description of the continuation coverage provided under the plan;
- An explanation of the steps qualified beneficiaries must take to notify the plan of qualifying events or disabilities;
- An explanation of the importance of keeping the plan administrator informed of addresses of the participants and beneficiaries; and
- A statement that the general notice does not fully describe COBRA or the plan and that more complete information is available from the plan administrator and in the SPD.

The Department of Labor has developed a model general notice that single-employer group health plans may use to satisfy the general notice requirement. In order to use this model general notice properly, the plan administrator (or employer if the employer administers COBRA) must complete it by filling in the blanks with the appropriate plan information. Use of the model general notice, appropriately completed, will be considered by the Department of Labor to be good faith compliance with the general notice content requirements of COBRA.

These and other sample notices are available on the book's website www.cobralawguide.com

The COBRA Qualifying Event Notice

Generally, a group health plan must offer continuation coverage to a qualified beneficiary upon the occurrence of a qualifying event. The group health plan is not required to act until it receives an appropriate notice of such a qualifying event. For the employer who self-administers COBRA, the plan and the employer are generally one and the same for purposes of COBRA administration.

If the employer does not administer COBRA, it is required to notify the plan if the qualifying event is:

- Termination or reduction in hours of employment of the covered employee;
- Death of the covered employee; or
- Covered employee's becoming entitled to Medicare.

The employer has 30 days after the event occurs to provide notice to the plan.

The covered employee or one of the qualified beneficiaries is responsible for notifying the plan if the qualifying event is:

- Divorce;
- Legal separation; or
- A child's loss of dependent status under the plan.

Thus, the obligation of notice on the part of the employer or plan for these three events listed above is triggered only when the covered employee or qualified beneficiary notifies the plan. Remember, however, that such obligation is premised on the assumption that the employer or plan appropriately previously provided the proper notices in the SPD and or the general notice. Again, these notices would have provided the covered employee and the qualified beneficiaries with the information he or she needed to: 1) understand under what circumstances the employer or plan needed to be notified; 2) how and when to make such notification; and 3) who to notify.

Group health plans are required to have procedures for how the covered employee or one of the qualified beneficiaries can provide notice of these types of qualifying events. The plan can set a time limit for providing this notice, but the time limit cannot be shorter than 60 days, starting from the latest of: (1) the date on which the qualifying event occurs; (2) the date on which the qualified beneficiary loses (or would lose) coverage under the plan as a result of the qualifying event; or (3) the date on which the qualified beneficiary is informed, through the furnishing of either the SPD or the COBRA general notice, of the responsibility to notify the plan and the procedures for doing so. The procedures must describe how, and to whom, notice should be given, and what information must be included in the qualifying event notice. If one person gives notice of a qualifying event, the notice covers all qualified beneficiaries affected by that event.

Be warned that if a group health plan does not have reasonable procedures for how to provide these notices, qualified beneficiaries are permitted to give notice (either written or oral) to the person or unit that handles the employer's employee benefits matters. If the plan is a multiemployer plan, notice can also be given to the joint board of trustees; and if the plan is administered by an insurance company (or the benefits are provided through insurance), notice can be given to the insurance company. If this occurs, it is anyone's guess as to how notice from a qualified beneficiary occurred. Thus, a carefully planned and communicated procedure is necessary in order to document each step.

The COBRA Election Notice

The COBRA Qualifying Event Notice is the notice that most think of when the subject of a COBRA notice comes up. Once the employer or plan receives notice of a qualifying event, the plan must provide the qualified beneficiaries with an election notice, which describes their rights to continuation coverage and how to make an election. The election notice must be provided to the qualified beneficiaries within 14 days after the plan administrator receives the notice of a qualifying event. Typically, for termination or reduction in hours, the notice must be provided within 14 days of the termination or reduction in hours. It is important to remember that if the employer is self-administering COBRA, it must provide the notice within the 14 days. If it relies on another party to administer COBRA, it must satisfy the notice requirements described above so that the plan administrator can provide timely notice. The election notice must include:

- The name of the plan and the name, address, and telephone number of the plan's COBRA administrator;
- Identification of the qualifying event;
- Identification of the qualified beneficiaries (by name or by status);
- An explanation of the qualified beneficiaries' right to elect continuation coverage;
- The date coverage will terminate (or has terminated) if continuation coverage is not elected;
- How to elect continuation coverage;
- What will happen if continuation coverage isn't elected or is waived;
- What continuation coverage is available, for how long, and (if it is for less than 36 months), how it can be extended for disability or second qualifying events;
- How continuation coverage might terminate early;
- Premium payment requirements, including due dates and grace periods;
- A statement of the importance of keeping the plan administrator informed of the addresses of qualified beneficiaries; and
- A statement that the election notice does not fully describe COBRA or the plan and that

more information is available from the plan administrator and in the SPD.

The Department of Labor has developed a model election notice that plans may use to satisfy their obligation to provide the election notice. Remember that to use the notice effectively it must be specifically tailored to follow the employer's or plan's processes. Use of the model election notice, appropriately completed, will be considered by the Department of Labor to be good faith compliance with the election notice content requirements of COBRA.

These and other sample notices are available on the book's website www.cobralawguide.com

The COBRA Notice of Unavailability of Continuation Coverage

Group health plans may sometimes deny a request for continuation coverage or for an extension of continuation coverage when the plan determines the requester is not entitled to receive it. This may occur, for example, when a family member was not enrolled on a health insurance plan and attempts to obtain COBRA coverage upon what it may erroneously believe was a qualifying event. When a group health plan makes the decision to deny a request for continuation coverage from an individual, the plan must give the individual a notice of unavailability of continuation coverage. The notice must be provided within 14 days after the request is received, and the notice must explain the reason for denying the request.

The COBRA Notice of Early Termination of Continuation Coverage

Continuation coverage must generally be made available for a maximum period (18, 29, or 36 months). The group health plan may terminate continuation coverage early, however, for any of a number of specific reasons, such as failure of payment, termination of the plan, etc.

When a group health plan decides to terminate continuation coverage early for any of these reasons, the plan must give the qualified beneficiary a notice of early termination. The notice must be given as soon as practicable after the decision is made, and it must describe the date coverage will terminate, the reason for termination, and any rights the qualified beneficiary may have under the plan or applicable law to elect alternative group or individual coverage, such as a right to convert to an individual policy.

Later in this guide is a comprehensive discussion of termination of COBRA coverage for which this notice would apply.

Special Rules for Multiemployer Plans

Multiemployer plans are allowed to adopt some special rules for COBRA notices. First, a multiemployer plan may adopt its own uniform time limits for the qualifying event notice or the election notice. A multiemployer plan also may choose not to require employers to provide qualifying event notices, and instead to have the plan administrator determine when a qualifying event has occurred.

Any special multiemployer plan rules must be set out in the plan's documents (and SPD), which, of course must be provided to plan participants.

3

COBRA Election Procedures

COBRA requires group health plans to give qualified beneficiaries an election period during which they can decide whether to elect continuation coverage. COBRA also gives qualified beneficiaries specific election rights. Generally, each qualified beneficiary must be given at least 60 days to choose whether or not to elect COBRA coverage, beginning from the later of the date the election notice is provided, or the date on which the qualified beneficiary would otherwise lose coverage under the group health plan due to the qualifying event. Thus, it is incumbent on administrators to provide the COBRA election notice timely. Failure to do so will extend the time that the qualified beneficiary will have to elect COBRA retroactively. The longer the delay, the greater the administrative headaches for the employer or administrator.

An election is considered to be made on the date it is sent to the plan administrator. If the election is made timely, coverage must be provided from the date that coverage would otherwise have been lost.

In the case of an indemnity or reimbursement arrangement, the employer or employee organization can provide for plan coverage during the election period or, if the plan allows retroactive reinstatement, the employer or employee organization can terminate the coverage of the qualified beneficiary and reinstate her or him when the election (and, if applicable, payment for the coverage) is made. Claims incurred by a qualified beneficiary during the election period do not have to be paid before the election (and, if applicable, payment for the coverage) is made. If a provider of health care (such as a physician, hospital, or pharmacy) contacts the plan to confirm coverage of a qualified beneficiary during the election period, the plan must give a complete response to the health care provider about the qualified beneficiary's COBRA continuation coverage rights during the election period. For example, if the plan provides coverage during the election period but cancels coverage retroactively if COBRA continuation coverage is not elected, then the plan must inform a provider that a qualified beneficiary for whom coverage has not been elected is covered but that the coverage is subject to retroactive termination. Similarly, if the plan cancels coverage but then retroactively reinstates it once COBRA continuation coverage is elected, then the plan must inform the provider that the qualified beneficiary currently does not have coverage but will have coverage retroactively to the date coverage was lost if COBRA continuation coverage is elected.

Each qualified beneficiary must be given an independent right to elect continuation coverage. This means that when several individuals (such as an employee, his or her spouse, and their dependent children) become qualified beneficiaries due to the same qualifying event, each individual can make a different choice among the available options. The plan must allow the covered employee or the covered employee's spouse to elect continuation coverage on behalf of all of the other qualified beneficiaries for the same qualifying event. A parent or legal guardian of a qualified beneficiary must also be allowed to elect on behalf of a minor child. As a result of this requirement, when an employee loses coverage as the result of a termination or reduction in hours, administrators will often send notices to each affected individual or to the employee "and family" so as to include those qualified beneficiaries that are not employees of the organization.

It is also important to know that even if a qualified beneficiary waives continuation coverage during the 60 day election period, he or she must also be permitted to later revoke the waiver of coverage and elect continuation coverage, as long as the revocation is done before the end of the election period. If a waiver is later revoked, however, the plan is permitted to make continuation coverage begin on the date the waiver was revoked. Waivers and revocations of waivers are considered made on the date they are sent to the employer, employee organization, or plan administrator, as applicable. Thus, the 60 day election period is always a period of uncertainty for the employer or administrator and careful record keeping is always required.

4

Benefits Available Under Continuation Coverage

Type of Coverage Provided

COBRA requires that the continuation coverage be identical to the coverage that is currently available under the plan to similarly situated individuals who are covered under the plan and not receiving continuation coverage. This is typically the same coverage that the qualified beneficiary had immediately before the qualifying event. A qualified beneficiary receiving continuation coverage must receive the same benefits, choices, and services that a similarly situated participant or beneficiary is currently receiving under the plan, such as the right during an open enrollment season to choose among available coverage options. The qualified beneficiary is also subject to the same plan rules and limits that would apply to a similarly situated participant or beneficiary, such as co-payment requirements, deductibles, and coverage limits. The plan's rules for filing benefit claims and appealing any claims denials also apply.

Any changes made to the plan's terms that apply to similarly situated active employees and their families will also apply to qualified beneficiaries receiving COBRA continuation coverage. If a child is born to or adopted by a covered employee during a period of continuation coverage, the child is automatically considered to be a qualified beneficiary receiving continuation coverage. The plan must allow the child to be added to the continuation coverage.

It is not at all uncommon for employers to change plan provisions during open enrollment periods and fail to notify COBRA participants of these changes. Therefore, it is important to remember that any changes in plan provisions for current employees will most likely affect the provisions for COBRA participants and proper notice must be given.

Maximum Length of COBRA Continuation Coverage

COBRA generally requires that continuation coverage extend from the date of the qualifying event for a limited period of time of either 18 or 36 months. The length of time for which continuation coverage must be made available (the "maximum period" of continuation coverage) depends on the type of qualifying event that gave rise to the COBRA rights.

When the qualifying event is the end of employment or reduction of the employee's hours, and the employee became entitled to Medicare less than 18 months before the qualifying event, COBRA coverage for the employee's spouse and dependents can last until 36 months after the date the employee becomes entitled to Medicare. For example, if a covered employee becomes entitled to Medicare 8 months before the date his/her employment ends (termination of employment is the COBRA qualifying event), COBRA coverage for his/her spouse and children would last 28 months (36 months minus 8 months).

When the qualifying event is the covered employee's termination of employment (for reasons other than gross misconduct) or reduction in hours of work, qualified beneficiaries must be provided a maximum of 18 months of continuation coverage. For all other qualifying events, qualified beneficiaries must be provided 36 months of continuation coverage.

To add complexity to the mix, an 18-month extension may be available to qualified beneficiaries receiving an 18-month maximum period of continuation coverage (giving a total maximum period of 36 months of continuation coverage) if the qualified beneficiaries experience a second qualifying event such as death of the covered employee, divorce or legal separation of the covered employee and spouse, Medicare entitlement, or loss of dependent child status under the plan. The second event can be a second qualifying event only if it would have caused the qualified beneficiary to lose coverage under the plan in the absence of the first qualifying event.

The plan must have procedures for how a notice of a second qualifying event should be provided, and these rules should be described in the plan's SPD (and in the election notice for any offer of an 18-month period of continuation coverage). The plan can set a time limit for providing this notice, but the time limit cannot be shorter than 60 days from the latest of: (1) the date on which the qualifying event occurs; (2) the date on which the qualified beneficiary loses (or would lose) coverage under the plan as a result of the qualifying event; or (3) the date on which the qualified beneficiary is informed, through the furnishing of either the SPD or the COBRA general notice, of the responsibility to notify the plan and the procedures for doing so.

Early Termination of COBRA Continuation Coverage

COBRA benefits do not last forever and there are several instances where coverage will end. The first, and least obvious to most, is when the employer stops providing a group health plan to its employees. Thus, once the employer stops offering coverage to its employees, the COBRA coverage ends as well.

If an individual fails to pay a premium payment timely, COBRA coverage will end. It is important to remember, however, that built into COBRA's protection is a 30 day grace period. In other words, if an individual pays the COBRA premium within 30 days of its due date, it is considered timely. This often poses administrative difficulties for employers in handling late payers.

Once the qualified beneficiary becomes eligible for another health plan (as an employee or otherwise) that does not contain a pre-existing condition limitation that applies to that individual, COBRA coverage for that qualified beneficiary ends.

In the case of an individual who is not a qualified beneficiary and who is receiving coverage under a group health plan solely because of the individual's relationship to a qualified beneficiary, if the plan's obligation to make COBRA continuation coverage available to the qualified beneficiary ceases under this section, the plan is not obligated to make coverage available to the individual who is not a qualified beneficiary.

COBRA coverage will also end when the qualified beneficiary becomes eligible for Medicare benefits. This topic is addressed in more detail later in Chapter 6.

If a qualified beneficiary first becomes covered under another group health plan (including for this purpose any group health plan of a governmental employer or employee organization) after the date on which CO-BRA continuation coverage is elected for the qualified beneficiary, then the plan may terminate the qualified beneficiary's COBRA continuation coverage upon the date on which the qualified beneficiary first becomes covered under the other group health plan (even if the other coverage is less valuable to the qualified beneficiary). By contrast, if a qualified beneficiary first becomes covered under another group health plan on or before the date on which COBRA continuation coverage is elected, then the other coverage cannot be a basis for terminating the qualified beneficiary's COBRA continuation coverage. This rule is satisfied if the qualified beneficiary is actually covered, rather than merely eligible to be covered, under the other group health plan and if the other group health plan does not contain any exclusion or limitation with respect to any pre-existing condition of the qualified.

Disability Extension of COBRA Continuation Coverage

If one of the qualified beneficiaries in a family is disabled and meets certain requirements described below, all of the qualified beneficiaries in that family are entitled to an 11-month extension of the maximum period of continuation coverage (for a total maximum period of 29 months of continuation coverage). The plan can charge qualified beneficiaries an increased premium, up to 150 percent of the cost of coverage, during the 11-month disability extension.

The requirements are that the disabled qualified beneficiary must be determined by the Social Security Administration (SSA) to be disabled at some time before the 60th day of continuation coverage and that the disability must continue during the rest of the initial 18-month period of continuation coverage.

The disabled qualified beneficiary (or another person on his or her behalf) must also notify the plan of the

SSA determination. The plan can set a time limit for providing this notice of disability, but the time limit cannot be shorter than 60 days, starting from the latest of: (1) the date on which SSA issues the disability determination; (2) the date on which the qualifying event occurs; (3) the date on which the qualified beneficiary loses (or would lose) coverage under the plan as a result of the qualifying event; or (4) the date on which the qualified beneficiary is informed, through the furnishing of either the SPD or the COBRA general notice, of the responsibility to notify the plan and the procedures for doing so.

The right to the disability extension may be terminated if SSA determines that the qualified beneficiary is no longer disabled, and the plan can require disabled qualified beneficiaries to provide notice when such a determination is made. The plan must give the qualified beneficiaries at least 30 days after the SSA determination in which to provide such notice.

The rules for how to give a disability notice and a notice of no longer being disabled should be described in the plan's SPD (and in the election notice for any offer of an 18-month period of continuation coverage).

Additional extensions of COBRA can be obtained in the following circumstances. If a qualifying event occurs that gives rise to an 18-month maximum coverage period (or a 29-month maximum coverage period in the case of a disability extension) is followed, within that 18-month period (or within that 29-month period, in the case of a disability extension), by a second qualifying event (for example, a death or a divorce) that gives rise to a 36-month maximum coverage period. Thus, a termination of employment following a qualifying event that is a reduction of hours of employment cannot be a second qualifying event that expands the maximum coverage period; the bankruptcy of an employer also cannot be a second qualifying event that expands the maximum coverage period. In such a case, the original 18-month period (or 29-month period, in the case of a disability extension) is expanded to 36 months, but only for those individuals who were qualified beneficiaries under the group health plan in connection with the first qualifying event and who are still qualified beneficiaries at the time of the second qualifying event. No qualifying event (other than a qualifying event that is the bankruptcy of the employer) can give rise to a maximum coverage period that ends more than 36 months after the date of the first qualifying event (or more than 36 months after the date of the loss of coverage, in the case of a plan that provides for the extension of the required periods). For example, if an employee covered by a group health plan that is subject to CO-BRA terminates employment (for reasons other than gross misconduct) on December 31, 2008, the termination is a qualifying event giving rise to a maximum coverage period that extends for 18 months to June 30, 2010. If the employee dies after the employee and the employee's spouse and dependent children have elected COBRA continuation coverage and on or before June 30, 2010, the spouse and dependent children (except anyone among them whose COBRA continuation coverage had already ended for some other reason) will be able to receive COBRA continuation coverage through December 31, 2011.

Conversion Options

Some health plans provide for what is called a conversion option. This option allows participants whose coverage ends under the plan to convert the employer plan to an individual plan. The general rule is that if a conversion option is available under the plan to active employees and their families, qualified beneficiaries whose maximum period of continuation coverage ends also must be given the option to convert to an individual policy. The conversion option must be offered not later than 180 days before continuation coverage ends. The option to convert, however, need not be provided if continuation coverage is terminated before the end of the maximum period for which it was made available.

5

Paying for Continuation Coverage

The maximum amount charged to qualified beneficiaries cannot exceed 102 percent of the cost to the plan (generally the monthly premium) for similarly situated individuals covered under the plan who have not incurred a qualifying event. In calculating premiums for continuation coverage, a plan can include the costs paid by the employee and the employer, plus an additional 2 percent for administrative costs. For disabled qualified beneficiaries receiving the 11-month disability extension of continuation coverage, the premium for those additional months may be increased to 150 percent of the plan's total cost of coverage.

COBRA charges to qualified beneficiaries may be increased if the cost to the plan increases but generally must be fixed in advance of each 12-month premium cycle. The plan must allow qualified beneficiaries to pay the required premiums on a monthly basis if they ask to do so, and may allow payments at other intervals (for example, weekly or quarterly).

Qualified beneficiaries cannot be required to pay a premium in connection with making the COBRA election. Plans must provide at least 45 days after the election (that is the date the qualified beneficiary mails the election form if using first-class mail) for making an initial premium payment. If a qualified beneficiary fails to make any payment before the end of the initial 45-day period, the plan can terminate the qualified beneficiary's COBRA rights. The plan should establish due dates for any premiums for subsequent periods of coverage, but as noted earlier, it must provide a minimum 30-day grace period for each payment.

As noted earlier, plans are permitted to terminate continuation coverage if full payment is not received before the end of a grace period. If the amount of a payment made to the plan is wrong, but is not significantly less (the lesser of $50 or 10 percent of the amount the plan requires to be paid) than the amount due, the plan must notify the qualified beneficiary of the deficiency and grant a reasonable period (for this purpose, 30 days is considered reasonable) to pay the difference. The plan is not obligated to send monthly premium notices, but is required to provide a notice of early termination if continuation coverage is terminated early due to failure to make a timely payment.

There are special rules for self-funded plans. These plans are permitted to select one of two options to calculate COBRA premiums – the Actuarially Determined Method or the Past Cost Method. These are complex rules and employers should therefore request that the insurance carrier provide the COBRA rates for plans with alternative funding schemes.

The Trade Adjustment Assistance Reform Act of 2002 (Trade Act of 2002) created the Health Coverage Tax Credit (HCTC), an advanceable, refundable tax credit for up to 65 percent of the premiums paid for specified types of health insurance coverage (including COBRA continuation coverage). The HCTC is available to certain workers who lose their jobs due to the effects of international trade and who qualify for trade adjustment assistance (TAA), as well as certain individuals who are receiving pension payments from the Pension Benefit Guaranty Corporation (PBGC). Individuals who are eligible for the HCTC may choose to have the amount of the credit paid on a monthly basis to their health coverage provider as it becomes due, or may claim the tax credit on their income tax returns at the end of the year. Appendix A describes the impact of the American Recovery and Reinvestment Act on those eligible for the HCTC.

PBGC-eligible individuals may be able to retain their COBRA coverage until death. The PBGC-eligible individual's spouse and dependents can keep the coverage for an additional 24 months beyond that. However, note that this provision, like the rest of the Trade

Adjustment Assistance Health Coverage Improvement Act, expires on December 31, 2010. At the time of this printing, these changes to the HCTC - including the new timeframes for extended benefits - are only valid through December 31, 2010.

6

Coordination with Other Federal Laws

COBRA and Medicare

If an individual qualifies for Medicare based upon age or disability, whether s/he can have both COBRA and Medicare depends on which s/he had first. If the individual already has COBRA when enrolling in Medicare, COBRA coverage will generally end on the date of enrollment in Medicare. Those who become Medicare eligible are typically advised to enroll in Medicare Part B immediately as they will not be entitled to a Medicare Special Enrollment Period when COBRA ends. The spouse and dependents of the individual may keep COBRA for up to 36 months when the affected individual enrolls in Medicare. One key exception to this rule is that individuals can keep COBRA for services that are not covered by Medicare such as, for example, dental coverage.

If an individual already has Medicare and then becomes eligible for COBRA, s/he must be allowed to enroll in COBRA. Unless qualification for Medicare was the result of End-Stage Renal Disease (ESRD). Medicare will act as the primary payer and COBRA will be the secondary payer. Those who typically enroll in COBRA are those whose plan benefits are more generous than the coverage provided by Medicare. Those who are eligible for Medicare because of ESRD are subject to a 30 month coordination period when the employer group health plan will pay first and Medicare will pay second. If an individual has COBRA during this time COBRA will be the primary insurance during the 30-month coordination period. If COBRA coverage ends before the 30 months have passed, Medicare becomes primary. If the individual still has COBRA when the 30-month coordination period ends, Medicare will pay first and COBRA coverage may end depending upon the laws in each particular state.

COBRA and HIPAA

The Health Insurance Portability and Accountability Act (HIPAA) requires that a group health plan or health insurance issuer provide a certificate of health coverage automatically to individuals entitled to elect COBRA continuation coverage, at a time no later than when a notice is required to be provided for a qualifying event under COBRA, and to individuals who elected COBRA coverage, either within a reasonable time after learning that the COBRA coverage has ceased, or within a reasonable time after the end of the grace period for payment of COBRA premiums.

Under HIPAA, upon certain events, group health plans and health insurance issuers are required to provide a special enrollment period during which an individual who previously declined coverage for themselves and/or their dependents may be allowed to enroll without having to wait until the next open season for enrollment, regardless of whether the plan has an open season or when the next open season begins. When an employee or dependent of an employee loses eligibility for other health coverage, a special enrollment right may be triggered. If the other health coverage was COBRA, special enrollment can be requested only after COBRA is exhausted.

Finally, under HIPAA, any pre-existing condition exclusion period that would apply under a group health plan or group health insurance coverage generally is reduced by an individual's number of days of creditable coverage that occurred without a break in coverage of 63 days or more. For this purpose, most health coverage, including COBRA coverage, is creditable coverage.

COBRA and the FMLA

The Internal Revenue Service issued regulations in January 2001 to address the interaction of COBRA and the Family and Medical Leave Act of 1993. The following general rules emerged from those regulations:

The taking of leave under FMLA does not constitute a qualifying event. However, a qualifying event will occur if: (a) An employee (or the spouse or a dependent child of the employee) is covered on the day before the first day of FMLA leave (or becomes covered during the FMLA leave) under a group health plan of the employee's employer; (b) The employee does not return to employment with the employer at the end of the FMLA leave; and (c) The employee (or the spouse or a dependent child of the employee) would, in the absence of COBRA continuation coverage, lose coverage under the group health plan before the end of the maximum coverage period. In this instance described above, the date of the qualifying event would be considered to be the last day of the employee's FMLA leave.

If an employee fails to pay the employee portion of premiums for coverage under a group health plan during FMLA leave or declines coverage under a group health plan during FMLA leave, this does not affect the determination of whether or when the employee has experienced a qualifying event. Any lapse of coverage under a group health plan during FMLA leave is irrelevant in determining whether a set of circumstances constitutes a qualifying event.

COBRA continuation coverage may not be conditioned upon reimbursement of the premiums paid by the employer for coverage under a group health plan during FMLA leave. Even if recovery of premiums during an individual's FMLA leave is made, the right to COBRA continuation coverage cannot be conditioned upon the employee's reimbursement to the employer for premiums the employer paid to maintain coverage under a group health plan during FMLA leave.

COBRA and USERRA

Reservists in the military who are called to active duty have certain rights which include the right to continued health insurance. While COBRA provides health coverage continuation rights to employees and their families after an event such as a reduction in employment hours, the Uniformed Services Employment and Reemployment Rights Act (USERRA) is intended to minimize the disadvantages that occur when a person needs to be absent from civilian employment to serve in the uniformed services.

Both COBRA and USERRA generally allow individuals who leave work for military service to continue coverage for themselves and their dependents under an employment-based group health plan. COBRA generally provides for 18 months of coverage, with further extensions for certain events described above. USERRA, which applies to all employers regardless of their size, provides for 24 months of coverage.

If military service is for 30 days or less, individuals and their families can continue their health insurance coverage at the same cost as before the service. If military service is longer, individuals and their families can be required to pay up to 102 percent of the full premium for coverage. Plans subject to COBRA should send COBRA notices to affected individuals.

APPENDIX A

ARRA's COBRA Subsidy as Amended by the Defense Act

The American Recovery and Reinvestment Act of 2009 (ARRA) permits "assistance eligible individuals" to pay reduced premiums and provides additional election opportunities for health benefits under the Consolidated Omnibus Budget Reconciliation Act (COBRA). These individuals will pay only 35% of the COBRA premium. 65% is paid by the employer (or Plan) and then reimbursed through a payroll tax credit. The reduction in premiums under ARRA applied to periods of health coverage beginning on or after February 17, 2009 and lasted for up to nine months. Both the Internal Revenue Service (IRS) and The United States Department of Labor (USDOL) provided information available on their websites.

The ARRA COBRA provisions are rather confusing. To make matters worse, at the end of 2009, ARRA's COBRA provisions were extended by the Department of Defense Appropriations Act for 2010 ("Defense Act"). Essentially the Defense Act does two things: it extends the period of eligibility and the length of the subsidy.

OVERVIEW OF THE COBRA SUBSIDY

The original COBRA subsidy under ARRA provided a nine month subsidy for COBRA continuation coverage for those who were *involuntarily* terminated AND *lost coverage as a result of a termination* within the period September 1, 2008 and December 1, 2009. Under the Defense Act, the expiration period of the subsidy is extended now for *fifteen* months through February 28, 2010. Thus, individuals are eligible for the extended subsidy if they are involuntarily terminated from employment beginning September 1, 2008 through February 28, 2010 and would be otherwise eligible for COBRA.

It is important to note that under the Defense Act, only the *termination from employment,* not the *loss of coverage* must occur before February 28, 2010. Thus, if an individual's employment is terminated prior to February 28th, but coverage does not terminate until *after* February 28th, s/he is eligible for the subsidy even though the loss of coverage occurred after the eligibility period.

Generally, under the original ARRA legislation, individuals who are eligible for other group health coverage (such as a spouse's plan) or Medicare are **not** eligible for the premium reduction and the subsidy is only available for premiums paid for periods of coverage after February 17, 2009.

An individual who pays the 35% COBRA premium is deemed to have paid the full COBRA premium. The remaining premium is taken as a credit by the employer/ plan against employment taxes. Credits which exceed the employment taxes owed are reimbursed. The IRS has revised Form 941 (Employer's Quarterly Federal Tax Return) accordingly.

Wage earners, with an adjusted gross income of over $145,000 (and joint filers with an adjusted gross income of over $290,000) for 2009 are not eligible for the subsidy. Those earning between $125,000 and $145,000 individually (and between $250,000 and $290,000 for joint filers) are subject to a "phase out" of the subsidy.

PLANS THAT ARE COVERED BY THE SUBSIDY

The COBRA premium reduction provisions apply to all group health plans sponsored by private-sector employers or employee organizations (unions) subject to the COBRA rules under the Employee Retirement Income Security Act of 1974 (ERISA) and the Internal Revenue Code. They also apply to plans sponsored by state or local governments subject to the continuation provisions under the Public Health Service Act, and plans in the Federal Employee Health Benefits Program (FEHBP). The premium reduction is also available for group health insurance that is required by State law to provide comparable continuation coverage (such as some "mini-COBRA" laws).

ELIGIBILITY

An "assistance eligible individual" is one who 1) has a COBRA qualifying event (or under a state COBRA law that provides comparable coverage) that relates to the employee's involuntary termination during the period between September 1, 2008 and February 28, 2010, and 2) makes a timely COBRA election. Individuals who are eligible for other group health coverage (such as a spouse's plan) or Medicare are *not* eligible for the premium reduction.

Individuals who have qualified and received the 65 percent subsidy for COBRA health insurance, due to involuntary termination from a prior job, are required to notify their former employer if they become eligible for other group health coverage since the subsidy is only available to those who have involuntarily lost their job and do not have coverage available elsewhere.

If an individual becomes eligible for other group health coverage, they should notify their plan in writing that they are no longer eligible for the CO-BRA subsidy. If an individual continues to receive the subsidy after they are eligible for other group health coverage, such as coverage from a new job or Medicare eligibility, the individual may be subject to the new IRC § 6720C penalty of 110 percent of the subsidy provided after they became eligible for the new coverage.

SWITCHING BENEFIT OPTIONS

If an employer offers additional coverage options to active employees, the employer may (but is not required to) allow assistance eligible individuals to switch the coverage options they had when they became eligible for COBRA. To retain eligibility for the ARRA premium reduction, the different coverage must have the same or lower premiums as the individual's original coverage. The different coverage cannot be coverage that provides only dental, vision, a health flexible spending account, or coverage for treatment that is furnished in an on-site facility maintained by the employer.

THE DEFENSE ACT's COBRA SUBSIDY EXTENSION IS RETROACTIVE

Under the Defense Act, any individual who previously had the federal COBRA subsidy but exhausted it after nine months will now have the opportunity to opt back into COBRA at the reduced subsidy rate for an additional six months (subject, of course, to the maximum COBRA continuation coverage period), retroactive to when s/he stopped paying for COBRA coverage.

If the individual remained on COBRA, exhausted the subsidy rate, and continued on COBRA by paying the higher, full-premium rate, s/he is entitled to a refund or credit of the excess premium paid retroactively.

In both of the above instances, the individuals must have paid their retroactive premiums by February

17, 2010 or 30 days after the notice of the extension is provided to them by the plan administrator.

THE DEFENSE ACT's NEW NOTICE REQUIRE- MENTS

The Defense Act requires that plan administrators provide a new notice to any individual who 1) was eligible for the ARRA COBRA subsidy on or after October 31, 2009, or 2) was voluntarily terminated on or after October 31, 2009. The notice must have been provided by February 17, 2010. Notice requirements for individuals who become eligible for COBRA after December 19, 2009 follow COBRA's traditional notice rules.

Additionally, notice must be given to those individuals who were eligible for the ARRA subsidy but either lost coverage for failure to pay premiums or who paid the full COBRA premiums after exhausting the subsidy.

Thus, if you have not done so, you should immediately send notice to any affected individuals by sending out a new COBRA notice and sample materials found on the USDOL's Website.

NEW NOTICES ARE AVAILABLE

The revised COBRA notices, available on the Department of Labor's website, are:

General Notice (Full version) – Send this notice to ALL qualified beneficiaries going forward. This combines a general COBRA notice with the premium reduction provisions of ARRA and the Defense Act.

<u>Premium Assistance Extension Notice</u> - Plan administrators must provide notice to certain individuals who have already been provided a COBRA General Notice that did not include information regarding the Defense Act. The following are the affected individuals that should receive this notice and the associated timing requirements:

Individuals who were "assistance eligible individuals" as of October 31, 2009 (unless they are in a transition period), and individuals who experienced a termination of employment on or after October 31, 2009 and lost health coverage (unless they were already provided a timely, updated General Notice). This notice must be provided by February 17, 2010.

DEFINITION OF THE TRANSITION PERIOD

Individuals who are in a "transition period" must be provided the Premium Assistance Extension Notice within 60 days of the first day of the transition period. An individual's "transition period" is the period that begins immediately after the end of the maximum number of months (generally nine) of premium reduction available under ARRA prior to its amendment. An individual is in a transition period only if the premium reduction provisions would continue to apply due to the extension from nine to 15 months and they otherwise remain eligible for the premium reduction. Individuals in a transition period must be provided notice of the extension within 60 days of the first day of their transition period. The notice must include information on the extension from nine to 15 months and the ability to make retroactive payments for certain unpaid reduced premiums. The transition period may include multiple periods of coverage. The retroactive payment(s) for the period(s) of coverage must have been made by the later of February 17, 2010, 30 days from when the notice was provided, or the end of the otherwise applicable payment grace period.

APPEALS PROCEDURES

If the plan determines that an individual is not eligible for the premium reduction, the affected individual can request an expedited review of the denial. The Department of Labor will handle requests related to private sector employer plans subject to ERISA's COBRA provisions. The Department of Health and Human Services will handle requests for federal, state, and local governmental employees, including public schools, public colleges and universities, or a police or fire department, as well as requests related to group health insurance coverage provided pursuant to state continuation coverage laws. The Departments are required to make a determination regarding such requests within 15 business days after receiving a completed application for review.

Appeals to the Department of Labor must be submitted on the U.S. Department of Labor application form. The form is available on the Department of Labor's website and can be completed online or mailed or faxed as indicated in the instructions.

TAA ELIGIBLE QUALIFIED BENEFICIARIES

The Trade Adjustment Assistance Health Coverage Improvement Act of 2009, enacted as part of ARRA, made changes to the Health Coverage Tax Credit.

The HCTC now pays a greater portion of an individual's health insurance. The tax credit has increased to 80 percent of qualified health insurance premiums. The 80 percent tax credit began in May 2009. Beginning in August 2009, newly-enrolled participants will see a credit on their HCTC account for qualified payments made in 2009 while enrolling in the HCTC Program.

The HCTC will be available to an individual's qualified family members for a longer period of time beginning in January 2010. They may continue receiving the HCTC for up to 24 months after the primary eligible individual enrolls in Medicare, gets divorced or dies.

COBRA coverage also is temporarily extended for HCTC-eligible individuals. TAA-eligible individuals can keep COBRA coverage as long as they continue to be TAA-eligible. Electing the COBRA premium reduction under ARRA disqualifies an individual for the HCTC. Individuals eligible for the HCTC will have received a notification from the IRS.

APPENDIX B

Final Rules Relating to Use of Electronic Communication and Recordkeeping Technologies by Employee Pension and Welfare Benefit Plans

These rules are provided to the reader for the purpose of explaining in detail the options for communicating electronically with plan participants in employee benefit plans.

DEPARTMENT OF LABOR
Pension and Welfare Benefits Administration
29 CFR Part 2520
RIN 1210-AA71
AGENCY: Pension and Welfare Benefits Administration, Department of Labor.
ACTION: Notice of final rulemaking.

SUMMARY: This document contains final rules under Title I of the Employee Retirement Income Security Act of 1974, as amended (ERISA), concerning the disclosure of certain employee benefit plan information through electronic media, and the maintenance and retention of employee benefit plan records in electronic form. The rules establish a safe harbor pursuant to which all pension and welfare benefit plans covered by Title I of ERISA may use electronic media to satisfy disclosure obligations under Title I of ERISA. The rules also provide standards concerning the use of electronic media in the maintenance and retention of records required by sections 107 and 209 of ERISA. The rules affect employee pension and welfare benefit plans, including group health plans, plan sponsors, administrators and fiduciaries, and plan participants and beneficiaries.

DATES: Effective Date: These regulations are effective October 9, 2002. Applicability Date: The requirements of Sec. 2520.107-1 apply as of the first day of the first plan year beginning on or after October 9, 2002.

Statutory Authority This regulation is issued pursuant to the authority in sections 104(b), 107, 209, and 505 of ERISA (Pub. L. 93-406, 88 Stat. 894, 29 U.S.C. 1027, 1059, 1134, 1135) and under Secretary of Labor's Order No.

1-87, 52 FR 13139, April 21, 1987. List of Subjects in 29 CFR Part 2520 Employee benefit plans, Employee Retirement Income Security Act, Pension plans, Recordkeeping, Welfare plans.

For the reasons set forth above, Part 2520 of Title 29 of the Code of Federal Regulations is amended as follows:

PART 2520--[AMENDED]

1. The authority for Part 2520 is revised to read as follows: Authority: Secs. 101, 102, 103, 104, 105, 107, 109, 110, 111(b)(2), 111(c), 209, and 505, Pub. L. 93-406, 88 Stat. 840-52, 865, 893 and 894 (29 U.S.C. 1021-1025, 1027, 1029-31, 1059, 1134 and 1135); Secretary of Labor's Order No. 27-74, 13-76, 1-87, and Labor Management Services Administration Order 2-6. Sections 2520.102-3, 2520.104b-1 and 2520.104b-3 also are issued under sec. 101(a), (c) and (g)(4) of Pub. L. 104-191, 110 Stat. 1936, 1939, 1951 and 1955 and, sec. 603 of Pub. L. 104-204, 110 Stat. 2935 (29 U.S.C. 1185 and 1191c). Sections 2520.104b-1 and 2520.107 are also issued under the authority of sec. 1510 of Pub. L. 105-37, 111 Stat. 1114.

2. Amend section 2520.104b-1 to revise the first sentence of paragraph (a), the first sentence of para-

graph (b)(1), and paragraph (c), and to add a new paragraph (e) to read as follows:

Sec. 2520.104b-1 Disclosure.

(a) General disclosure requirements.

The administrator of an employee benefit plan covered by Title I of the Act must disclose certain material, including reports, statements, notices, and other documents, to participants, beneficiaries and other specified individuals. Disclosure under Title I of the Act generally takes three forms.

(b) Fulfilling the disclosure obligation.

> (1) Except as provided in paragraph (e) of this section, where certain material, including reports, statements, notices and other documents, is required under Title I of the Act, or regulations issued thereunder, to be furnished either by direct operation of law or on individual request, the plan administrator shall use measures reasonably calculated to ensure actual receipt of the material by plan participants, beneficiaries and other specified individuals.

(c) Disclosure through electronic media.

> (1) Except as otherwise provided by applicable law, rule or regulation, the administrator of an employee benefit plan furnishing documents through electronic media is deemed to satisfy the requirements of paragraph (b)(1) of this

section with respect to an individual described in paragraph (c)(2) if:

(i) The administrator takes appropriate and necessary measures reasonably calculated to ensure that the system for furnishing documents-- (A) Results in actual receipt of transmitted information (e.g., using return-receipt or notice of undelivered electronic mail features, conducting periodic reviews or surveys to confirm receipt of the transmitted information); and (B) Protects the confidentiality of personal information relating to the individual's accounts and benefits (e.g., incorporating into the system measures designed to preclude unauthorized receipt of or access to such information by individuals other than the individual for whom the information is intended);

(ii) The electronically delivered documents are prepared and furnished in a manner that is consistent with the style, format and content requirements applicable to the particular document;

(iii) Notice is provided to each participant, beneficiary or other individual, in electronic or non-electronic form, at the time a document is furnished electronically, that apprises the individual of the significance of the document when it is not otherwise reasonably evident as transmitted (e.g., the attached document describes changes in the benefits provided by your plan)and of the right to request and obtain a paper version of such document; and

(iv) Upon request, the participant, beneficiary or other individual is furnished a paper version of the electronically furnished documents.

(2) Paragraph (c)(1) shall only apply with respect to the following individuals:

(i) A participant who-- (A) Has the ability to effectively access documents furnished in electronic form at any location where the participant is reasonably expected to perform his or her duties as an employee; and (B) With respect to whom access to the employer's or plan sponsor's electronic information system is an integral part of those duties; or

(ii) A participant, beneficiary or any other person entitled to documents under Title I of the Act or regulations issued thereunder (including, but not limited to, an ``alternate payee'' within the meaning of section 206(d)(3) of the Act and a ``qualified beneficiary'' within the meaning of section 607(3) of the Act) who-- (A) Except as provided in paragraph (c)(2)(ii)(B) of this section, has affirmatively consented, in electronic or non-electronic form, to receiving documents through electronic media and has not withdrawn such consent; (B) In the case of documents to be furnished through the Internet or other electronic communication network, has affirmatively consented or confirmed consent electronically, in a manner that reasonably demonstrates the individual's ability to access information in the electronic form that will be used to provide the information that is the subject of the consent, and has provided an address for the receipt of electronically furnished documents; (C) Prior to consenting, is provided, in electronic or non-electronic form, a clear and conspicuous statement indicating: (1) The types of documents to which the consent would apply; (2) That consent can be withdrawn at any time without charge; (3) The procedures for withdrawing consent and for updating the participant's, beneficiary's or other individual's address for receipt of electronically furnished documents or other information; (4) The right to request and obtain a paper version of an electronically furnished document, including whether the paper version will be provided free of charge; and (5) Any hardware and software requirements for accessing and retaining the documents; and (D) Following consent, if a change in hardware or software requirements needed to access or retain electronic documents creates a material risk that the individual will be unable to access or retain electronically furnished documents: (1) Is provided with a statement of the revised hardware or software requirements for access to and retention of electronically furnished documents; (2) Is given the right to withdraw consent without charge and without the imposition of any condition or consequence that was not disclosed at the time of the initial consent; and (3) Again consents, in accordance with the requirements of paragraph (c)(2)(ii)(A) or paragraph (c)(2)(ii)(B) of this section, as applicable, to the receipt of documents through electronic media. (e) Limitations. This section does not apply to disclosures required under provisions of part 2 and part 3 of the Act over which the Secretary of the Treasury has interpretative and regulatory authority pursuant to Reorganization Plan No. 4 of 1978.

3. Add subpart G to part 2520 to read as follows: Subpart G--Recordkeeping Requirements

Sec. 2520.107-1 Use of electronic media for maintenance and retention of records.

(a) Scope and purpose. Sections 107 and 209 of the Employee Retirement Income Security Act of 1974, as amended (ERISA), contain certain requirements relating to the maintenance of records for reporting and disclosure purposes and for determining the pension benefits to which participants and beneficiaries are or may become entitled. This section provides standards applicable to both pension and welfare plans concerning the use of electronic media for the maintenance and retention of records required to be kept under sections 107 and 209 of ERISA.

(b) General requirements. The record maintenance and retention requirements of sections 107 and 209 of ERISA are satisfied when using electronic media if:

> (1) The electronic recordkeeping system has reasonable controls to ensure the integrity, accuracy, authenticity and reliability of the records kept in electronic form;

> (2) The electronic records are maintained in reasonable order and in a safe and accessible place, and in such manner as they may be readily inspected or examined (for example, the recordkeeping system should be capable of indexing, retaining, preserving, retrieving and reproducing the electronic records);

> (3) The electronic records are readily convertible into legible and readable paper copy as may be needed to satisfy reporting and disclosure requirements or any other obligation under Title I of ERISA;

> (4) The electronic recordkeeping system is not subject, in whole or in part, to any agreement or restriction that would, directly or indirectly,

compromise or limit a person's ability to comply with any reporting and disclosure requirement or any other obligation under Title I of ERISA; and (5) Adequate records management practices are established and implemented (for example, following procedures for labeling of electronically maintained or retained records, providing a secure storage environment, creating back-up electronic copies and selecting an off-site storage location, observing a quality assurance program evidenced by regular evaluations of the electronic recordkeeping system including periodic checks of electronically maintained or retained records, and retaining paper copies of records that cannot be clearly, accurately or completely transferred to an electronic recordkeeping system).

(c) Legibility and readability. All electronic records must exhibit a high degree of legibility and readability when displayed on a video display terminal or other method of electronic transmission and when reproduced in paper form. The term ``legibility'' means the observer must be able to identify all letters and numerals positively and quickly to the exclusion of all other letters or numerals. The term ``readability'' means that the observer must be able to recognize a group of letters or numerals as words or complete numbers.

(d) Disposal of original paper records. Original paper records may be disposed of any time after they are transferred to an electronic recordkeeping system that complies with the requirements of this section, except such original records may not be discarded if the electronic record would not constitute a duplicate or substitute record under the terms of the plan and applicable federal or state law.

Signed at Washington, D.C., this 3rd day of April, 2002.

Ann L. Combs, Assistant Secretary, Pension and Welfare Benefits, Administration, Department of Labor.

[FR Doc. 02-8499 Filed 4-8-02; 8:45 am]

BILLING CODE 4510-29-P

APPENDIX C

Health Care Continuation Coverage Final Notice Rules

The author has included these regulations specifically in order to provide the necessary details to readers who are self-administering COBRA. These regulations provide the necessary details and requirements of the notices that are required for proper COBRA administration. In addition, they explain the where the appropriate responsibility lies for certain areas of communication and administration.

Subchapter L--Group Health Plans

PART 2590--RULES AND REGULATIONS FOR GROUP HEALTH PLANS

Sec. 2590.606-1. General notice of continuation coverage.

(a) General. Pursuant to section 606(a)(1) of the Employee Retirement Income Security Act of 1974, as amended (the Act), the administrator of a group health plan subject to the continuation coverage requirements of part 6 of title I of the Act shall provide, in accordance with this section, written notice to each covered employee and spouse of the covered employee (if any) of the right to continuation coverage provided under the plan.

(b) Timing of notice. (1) The notice required by paragraph (a) of this section shall be furnished to each employee and each employee's spouse, not later than the earlier of:

(i) The date that is 90 days after the date on which such individual's coverage under the plan commences, or, if later, the date that is 90 days after the date on which the plan first becomes subject to the continuation coverage requirements; or

(ii) The first date on which the administrator is required, pursuant to Sec. 2590.606-4(b), to furnish the covered employee, spouse, or dependent child of such employee notice of a qualified beneficiary's right to elect continuation coverage.

(2) A notice that is furnished in accordance with paragraph (b)(1) of this section shall, for purposes of section 606(a)(1) of the Act, be deemed to be provided at the time of commencement of coverage under the plan.

(3) In any case in which an administrator is required to furnish a notice to a covered employee or spouse pursuant to paragraph (b)(1)(ii) of this section, the furnishing of a notice to such individual in accordance with Sec. 2590.606-4(b) shall be deemed to satisfy the requirements of this section.

(c) Content of notice. The notice required by paragraph (a) of this section shall be written in a manner calculated to be understood by the average plan participant and shall contain the following information:

(1) The name of the plan under which continuation coverage is available, and the name, address and telephone number of a party or parties from whom additional information about the plan and continuation coverage can be obtained;

(2) A general description of the continuation coverage under the plan, including identification of the classes of individuals who may become qualified beneficiaries, the types of qualifying events that may give rise to the right to continuation coverage, the obligation of the employer to notify the plan administrator of the occurrence of certain qualifying events, the maximum period for which continuation coverage may be available, when and under what circumstances continuation coverage may be extended beyond the applicable maximum period, and the

plan's requirements applicable to the payment of premiums for continuation coverage;

(3) An explanation of the plan's requirements regarding the responsibility of a qualified beneficiary to notify the administrator of a qualifying event that is a divorce, legal separation, or a child's ceasing to be a dependent under the terms of the plan, and a description of the plan's procedures for providing such notice;

(4) An explanation of the plan's requirements regarding the responsibility of qualified beneficiaries who are receiving continuation coverage to provide notice to the administrator of a determination by the Social Security Administration, under title II or XVI of the Social Security Act (42 U.S.C. 401 et seq. or 1381 et seq.), that a qualified beneficiary is disabled, and a description of the plan's procedures for providing such notice;

(5) An explanation of the importance of keeping the administrator informed of the current addresses of all participants or beneficiaries under the plan who are or may become qualified beneficiaries; and

(6) A statement that the notice does not fully describe continuation coverage or other rights under the plan and that more complete information regarding such rights is available from the plan administrator and in the plan's SPD.

(d) Single notice rule. A plan administrator may satisfy the requirement to provide notice in accordance with this section to a covered employee and the covered employee's spouse by furnishing a single notice addressed to both the covered employee and the covered employee's spouse, if, on the basis of the most recent information available to the plan, the covered employee's spouse resides at the same location as the covered employee, and the spouse's coverage under the plan commences on or after the date on which the covered employee's coverage commences, but not later than the date on which the notice required by this section is required to be provided to the covered employee. Nothing in this section shall be construed to create a requirement to provide a separate notice to dependent children who share a residence with a covered employer or a covered employee's spouse to whom notice is provided in accordance with this section.

(e) Notice in summary plan description. A plan administrator may satisfy the requirement to provide notice in accordance with this section by including the information described in paragraphs (c)(1), (2), (3), (4), and (5) of this section in a summary plan description meeting the requirements of Sec. 2520.102-3 of this chapter furnished in accordance with paragraph (b) of this section.

(f) Delivery of notice. The notice required by this section shall be furnished in a manner consistent with the requirements of Sec. 2520.104b-1 of this chapter, including paragraph (c) of that section relating to the use of electronic media.

(g) Model notice. The appendix to this section contains a model notice that is intended to assist administrators in discharging the notice obligations of this section. Use of the model notice is not mandatory. The model notice reflects the requirements of this section as they would apply to single-employer group health plans and must be modified if used to provide notice with respect to other types of group health plans, such as multiemployer plans or plans established and maintained by employee organizations for their members. In order to use the model notice, administrators must appropriately add relevant information where indicated in the model notice, select among alternative language, and supplement the model notice to reflect applicable plan provisions. Items of information that are not applicable to a particular plan may be deleted. Use of the model notice, appropriately modified and supplemented, will be deemed to satisfy the notice content requirements of paragraph (c) of this section.

(h) Applicability. This section shall apply to any notice obligation described in this section that arises on or after the first day of the first plan year beginning on or after November 26, 2004.

Sec. 2590.606-2. Notice requirement for employers.

(a) General. Pursuant to section 606(a)(2) of the Employee Retirement Income Security Act of 1974, as amended (the Act), except as otherwise provided herein, the employer of a covered employee under a group health plan subject to the continuation coverage requirements of part 6 of title I of the Act shall provide, in accordance with this section, notice to the administrator of the plan of the occurrence of a qualifying event that is the covered employee's death, termination of employment (other than by reason of gross misconduct), reduction in hours of employment, Medicare entitlement, or a proceeding in a case under title 11, United States Code, with respect to the employer from whose employment the covered employee retired at any time.

(b) Timing of notice. The notice required by this section shall be furnished to the administrator of the plan--

(1) In the case of a plan that provides, with respect to a qualifying event, pursuant to section 607(5) of the Act, that continuation coverage and the applicable period for providing notice under section 606(a)(2) of the Act shall commence on the date of loss of coverage, not later than 30 days after the date on which a qualified beneficiary loses coverage under the plan due to the qualifying event;

(2) In the case of a multiemployer plan that provides, pursuant to section 606(a)(2) of the Act, for a longer period of time within which employers may provide notice of a qualifying event, not later than the end of the period provided pursuant to the plan's terms for such notice; and

(3) In all other cases, not later than 30 days after the date on which the qualifying event occurred.

(c) Content of notice. The notice required by this section shall include sufficient information to enable the administrator to determine the plan, the covered employee, the qualifying event, and the date of the qualifying event.

(d) Multiemployer plan special rules. This section shall not apply to any employer that maintains a multiemployer plan, with respect to qualifying events affecting coverage under such plan, if the plan provides, pursuant to section 606(b) of the Act, that the administrator shall determine whether such a qualifying event has occurred.

(e) Applicability. This section shall apply to any notice obligation described in this section that arises on or after the first day of the first plan year beginning on or after November 26, 2004.

Sec. 2590.606-3. Notice requirements for covered employees and qualified beneficiaries.

(a) General. In accordance with the authority of sections 505 and 606(a)(3) of the Employee Retirement Income Security Act of 1974, as amended (the Act), this section sets forth requirements for group health plans subject to the continuation coverage requirements of part 6 of title I of the Act with respect to the responsibility of covered employees and qualified beneficiaries to provide the following notices to administrators:

(1) Notice of the occurrence of a qualifying event that is a divorce or legal separation of a covered employee from his or her spouse;

(2) Notice of the occurrence of a qualifying event that is a beneficiary's ceasing to be covered under a plan as a dependent child of a participant;

(3) Notice of the occurrence of a second qualifying event after a qualified beneficiary has become entitled to continuation coverage with a maximum duration of 18 (or 29) months;

(4) Notice that a qualified beneficiary entitled to receive continuation coverage with a maximum duration of 18 months has been determined by the Social Security Administration, under title II or XVI of the Social Security Act (42 U.S.C. 401 et seq. or 1381 et seq.) (SSA), to be disabled at any time during the first 60 days of continuation coverage; and

(5) Notice that a qualified beneficiary, with respect to whom a notice described in paragraph (a)(4) of this section has been provided, has subsequently been determined by the Social Security Administration, under title II or XVI of the SSA to no longer be disabled.

(b) Reasonable procedures. (1) A plan subject to the continuation coverage requirements shall establish reasonable procedures for the furnishing of the notices described in paragraph (a) of this section.

(2) For purposes of this section, a plan's notice procedures shall be deemed reasonable only if such procedures:

(i) Are described in the plan's summary plan description required by Sec. 2520.102-3 of this chapter;

(ii) Specify the individual or entity designated to receive such notices;

(iii) Specify the means by which notice may be given;

(iv) Describe the information concerning the qualifying event or determination of disability that the plan deems necessary in order to provide continuation coverage rights consistent with the requirements of the Act; and

(v) Comply with the requirements of paragraphs (c), (d), and (e) of this section.

(3) A plan's procedures will not fail to be reasonable, pursuant to this section, solely because the procedures require a covered employee or qualified beneficiary to utilize a specific form to provide notice to the administrator, provided that any such form is easily available, without cost, to covered employees and qualified beneficiaries.

(4) If a plan has not established reasonable procedures for providing a notice required by this section, such notice shall be deemed to have been provided when a written or oral communication identifying a specific event is made in a manner reasonably calculated to bring the information to the attention of any of the following:

(i) In the case of a single-employer plan, the person or organizational unit that customarily handles employee benefits matters of the employer;

(ii) In the case of a plan to which more than one unaffiliated employer contributes, or which is established or maintained by an employee organization, either the joint board, association, committee, or other similar group (or any member of any such group) administering the plan, or the person or organizational unit to which claims for benefits under the plan customarily are referred; or

(iii) In the case of a plan the benefits of which are provided or administered by an insurance company, insurance service, or other similar organization subject to regulation under the insurance laws of one or more States, the person or organizational unit that customarily handles claims for benefits under the plan or any officer of the insurance company, insurance service, or other similar organization.

(c) Periods of time for providing notice. A plan may establish a reasonable period of time for furnishing any of the notices described in paragraph (a) of this section, provided that any time limit imposed by the plan with respect to a particular notice may not be shorter than the time limit described in this paragraph (c) with respect to that notice.

(1) Time limits for notices of qualifying events. The period of time for furnishing a notice described in paragraph (a)(1), (2), or (3) of this section may not end before the date that is 60 days after the latest of:

(i) The date on which the relevant qualifying event occurs;

(ii) The date on which the qualified beneficiary loses (or would lose) coverage under the plan as a result of the qualifying event; or

(iii) The date on which the qualified beneficiary is informed, through the furnishing of the plan's summary plan description or the notice described in Sec. 2590.606-1, of both the responsibility to provide the notice and the plan's procedures for providing such notice to the administrator.

(2) Time limits for notice of disability determination. (i) Subject to paragraph (c)(2)(ii) of this section, the period of time for furnishing the notice described in paragraph (a)(4) of this section may not end before the date that is 60 days after the latest of:

(A) The date of the disability determination by the Social Security Administration;

(B) The date on which a qualifying event occurs;

(C) The date on which the qualified beneficiary loses (or would lose) coverage under the plan as a result of the qualifying event; or

(D) The date on which the qualified beneficiary is informed, through the furnishing of the summary plan description or the notice described in Sec. 2590.606-1, of both the responsibility to provide the notice and the plan's procedures for providing such notice to the administrator.

(ii) Notwithstanding paragraph (c)(2)(i) of this section, a plan may require the notice described in paragraph (a)(4) of this section to be furnished before the end of the first 18 months of continuation coverage.

(3) Time limits for notice of change in disability status. The period of time for furnishing the notice described in paragraph (a)(5) of this section may not end before the date that is 30 days after the later of:

(i) The date of the final determination by the Social Security Administration, under title II or XVI of the SSA, that the qualified beneficiary is no longer disabled; or

(ii) The date on which the qualified beneficiary is informed, through the furnishing of the plan's summary plan description or the notice described in Sec. 2590.606-1, of both the responsibility to provide the notice and the plan's procedures for providing such notice to the administrator.

(d) Required contents of notice. (1) A plan may establish reasonable requirements for the content of any notice described in this section, provided that a plan may not deem a notice to have been provided untimely if such notice, although not containing all of the information required by the plan, is provided within the time limit established under the plan in conformity with paragraph (c) of this section, and the administrator is able to determine from such notice the plan, the covered employee and qualified beneficiary(ies), the qualifying event or disability, and the date on which the qualifying event (if any) occurred.

(2) An administrator may require a notice that does not contain all of the information required by the plan to be supplemented with the additional information necessary to meet the plan's reasonable content requirements for such notice in order for the

notice to be deemed to have been provided in accordance with this section.

(e) Who may provide notice. With respect to each of the notice requirements of this section, any individual who is either the covered employee, a qualified beneficiary with respect to the qualifying event, or any representative acting on behalf of the covered employee or qualified beneficiary may provide the notice, and the provision of notice by one individual shall satisfy any responsibility to provide notice on behalf of all related qualified beneficiaries with respect to the qualifying event.

(f) Plan provisions. To the extent that a plan provides a covered employee or qualified beneficiary a period of time longer than that specified in this section to provide notice to the administrator, the terms of the plan shall govern the time frame for such notice.

(g) Additional rights to continuation coverage. Nothing in this section shall be construed to preclude a plan from providing, in accordance with its terms, continuation coverage to a qualified beneficiary although a notice requirement of this section was not satisfied.

(h) Applicability. This section shall apply to any notice obligation described in this section that arises on or after the first day of the first plan year beginning on or after November 26, 2004.

Sec. 2590.606-4. Notice requirements for plan administrators.

(a) General. Pursuant to section 606(a)(4) of the Employee Retirement Income Security Act of 1974, as amended (the Act), the administrator of a group health plan subject to the continuation coverage requirements of Part 6 of title I of the Act shall provide, in accordance with this section, notice to each qualified beneficiary of the qualified beneficiary's rights to continuation coverage under the plan.

(b) Notice of right to elect continuation coverage. (1) Except as provided in paragraph (b) (2) or (3) of this section, upon receipt of a notice of qualifying event furnished in accordance with Sec. 2590.606-2 or Sec. 2590.606-3, the administrator shall furnish to each qualified beneficiary, not later than 14 days after receipt of the notice of qualifying event, a notice meeting the requirements of paragraph (b)(4) of this section.

(2) In the case of a plan with respect to which an employer of a covered employee is also the administrator of the plan, except as provided in paragraph (b)(3) of this section, if the employer is otherwise required to furnish a notice of a qualifying event to an administrator pursuant to Sec. 2590.606-2, the administrator shall furnish to each qualified beneficiary a notice meeting the requirements of paragraph (b)(4) of this section not later than 44 days after:

(i) In the case of a plan that provides, with respect to the qualifying event, that continuation coverage and the applicable period for providing notice under section 606(a)(2) of the Act shall commence with the date of loss of coverage, the date on which a qualified beneficiary loses coverage under the plan due to the qualifying event; or

(ii) In all other cases, the date on which the qualifying event occurred.

(3) In the case of a plan that is a multiemployer plan, a notice meeting the requirements of paragraph (b)(4) of this section shall be furnished not later than the later of:

(i) The end of the time period provided in paragraph (b)(1) of this section; or

(ii) The end of the time period provided in the terms of the plan for such purpose.

(4) The notice required by this paragraph (b) shall be written in a manner calculated to be understood by the average plan participant and shall contain the following information:

(i) The name of the plan under which continuation coverage is available; and the name, address and telephone number of the party responsible under the plan for the administration of continuation coverage benefits;

(ii) Identification of the qualifying event;

(iii) Identification, by status or name, of the qualified beneficiaries who are recognized by the plan as being entitled to elect continuation coverage with respect to the qualifying event, and the date on which coverage under the plan will terminate (or has terminated) unless continuation coverage is elected;

(iv) A statement that each individual who is a qualified beneficiary with respect to the qualifying event has an independent right to elect continuation coverage, that a covered employee or a qualified beneficiary who is the spouse of the covered employee (or was the spouse of the covered employee on the day before the qualifying event occurred) may elect continuation coverage on behalf of all other qualified beneficiaries with respect to the qualifying event, and that a parent or legal guardian may elect continuation coverage on behalf of a minor child;

(v) An explanation of the plan's procedures for electing continuation coverage, including an explanation of the time period during which the election must be made, and the date by which the election must be made;

(vi) An explanation of the consequences of failing to elect or waiving continuation coverage, including an explanation that a qualified beneficiary's decision whether to elect continuation coverage will affect the future rights of qualified beneficiaries to portability of group health coverage, guaranteed access to individual health coverage, and special enrollment under part 7 of title I of the Act, with a reference to where a qualified beneficiary may obtain additional information about such rights; and a description of the plan's procedures for revoking a waiver of the right to continuation coverage before the date by which the election must be made;

(vii) A description of the continuation coverage that will be made available under the plan, if elected, including the date on which such coverage will commence, either by providing a description of the coverage or by reference to the plan's summary plan description;

(viii) An explanation of the maximum period for which continuation coverage will be available under the plan, if elected; an explanation of the continuation coverage termination date; and an explanation of any events that might cause continuation coverage to be terminated earlier than the end of the maximum period;

(ix) A description of the circumstances (if any) under which the maximum period of continuation coverage may be extended due either to the occurrence of a second qualifying event or a determination by the Social Security Administration, under title II or XVI of the Social Security Act (42 U.S.C. 401 et seq. or 1381 et seq.) (SSA), that the qualified beneficiary is disabled, and the length of any such extension;

(x) In the case of a notice that offers continuation coverage with a maximum duration of less than 36 months, a description of the plan's requirements regarding the responsibility of qualified beneficiaries to provide notice of a second qualifying event and notice of a disability determination under the SSA, along with a description of the plan's procedures for providing such notices, including the times within which such notices must be provided and the consequences of failing to provide such notices. The notice shall also explain the responsibility of qualified beneficiaries to provide notice that a disabled qualified beneficiary has subsequently been determined to no longer be disabled;

(xi) A description of the amount, if any, that each qualified beneficiary will be required to pay for continuation coverage;

(xii) A description of the due dates for payments, the qualified beneficiaries' right to pay on a monthly basis, the grace periods for payment, the address to which payments should be sent, and the consequences of delayed payment and non-payment;

(xiii) An explanation of the importance of keeping the administrator informed of the current addresses of all participants or beneficiaries under the plan who are or may become qualified beneficiaries; and

(xiv) A statement that the notice does not fully describe continuation coverage or other rights under the plan, and that more complete information regarding such rights is available in the plan's summary plan description or from the plan administrator.

(c) Notice of unavailability of continuation coverage. (1) In the event that an administrator receives a notice furnished in accordance with Sec. 2590.606-3 relating to a qualifying event, second qualifying event, or determination of disability by the Social Security Administration regarding a covered employee, qualified beneficiary, or other individual and determines that the individual is not entitled to continuation coverage under part 6 of title I of the Act, the administrator shall provide to such individual an explanation as to why the individual is not entitled to continuation coverage.

(2) The notice required by this paragraph (c) shall be written in a manner calculated to be understood by the average plan participant and shall be furnished by the administrator in accordance with the time frame set out in paragraph (b) of this section that would apply if the administrator received a notice of qualifying event and determined that the individual was entitled to continuation coverage.

(d) Notice of termination of continuation coverage. (1) The administrator of a plan that is providing continuation coverage to one or more qualified beneficiaries with respect to a qualifying event shall provide, in accordance with this paragraph (d), notice to each such qualified beneficiary of any termination of continuation coverage that takes effect earlier than the end of the maximum period of continuation coverage applicable to such qualifying event.

(2) The notice required by this paragraph (d) shall be written in a manner calculated to be understood by the average plan participant and shall contain the following information:

(i) The reason that continuation coverage has terminated earlier than the end of the maximum period of continuation coverage applicable to such qualifying event;

(ii) The date of termination of continuation coverage; and

(iii) Any rights the qualified beneficiary may have under the plan or under applicable law to elect an alternative group or individual coverage, such as a conversion right.

(3) The notice required by this paragraph (d) shall be furnished by the administrator as soon as practicable following the administrator's determination that continuation coverage shall terminate.

(e) Special notice rules. The notices required by paragraphs (b), (c), and (d) of this section shall be furnished to each qualified beneficiary or individual, except that:

(1) An administrator may provide notice to a covered employee and the covered employee's spouse by furnishing a single notice addressed to both the covered employee and the covered employee's spouse, if, on the basis of the most recent information available to the plan, the covered employee's spouse resides at the same location as the covered employee; and

(2) An administrator may provide notice to each qualified beneficiary who is the dependent child of a covered employee by furnishing a single notice to the covered employee or the covered employee's spouse, if, on the basis of the most recent information available to the plan, the dependent child resides at the same location as the individual to whom such notice is provided.

(f) Delivery of notice. The notices required by this section shall be furnished in any manner consistent with the requirements of Sec. 2520.104b-1 of this chapter, including paragraph (c) of that section relating to the use of electronic media.

(g) Model notice. The appendix to this section contains a model notice that is intended to assist administrators in discharging the notice obligations of paragraph (b) of this section. Use of the model notice is not mandatory. The model notice reflects the requirements of this section as they would apply to single-employer group health plans and must be modified if used to provide notice with respect to other types of group health plans, such as multiemployer plans or plans established and maintained by employee organizations for their members. In order to use the model notice, administrators must appropriately add relevant information where indicated in the model notice, select among alternative language and supplement the model notice to reflect applicable plan provisions. Items of information that are not applicable to a particular plan may be deleted. Use of the model notice, appropriately modified and supplemented, will be deemed to satisfy the notice content requirements of paragraph (b)(4) of this section.

(h) Applicability. This section shall apply to any notice obligation described in this section that arises on or after the first day of the first plan year beginning on or after November 26, 2004.

Signed at Washington, DC., this 19th day of May, 2004.

Ann L. Combs, Assistant Secretary, Employee Benefits Security Administration, Department of Labor.

[FR Doc. 04-11796 Filed 5-25-04; 8:45 am]

APPENDIX D

PWBA Office of Regulations and Interpretations

Advisory Opinion

November 10, 1999

Mr. Pieter J. Doerr
COBRA Compliance Systems, Inc.
15 E. Washington Street
P.O. Box 889
Coldwater, Michigan 49036-0889

Dear Mr. Doerr:

This is in reply to your request for an advisory opinion regarding the continuation coverage provisions applicable to group health plans under Part 6 of Title I of the Employee Retirement Income Security Act of 1974, as amended (ERISA).

Under Part 6, which was added to ERISA by the Consolidated Omnibus Budget Reconciliation Act of 1985 (COBRA), group health plans are required to offer temporary extension of health coverage (called "COBRA continuation coverage") at group rates to employees, spouses and dependent children in certain instances where their coverage under the plan would otherwise end.1 Section 606(a)(1) of Title I of ERISA provides that the covered employee and his or her covered spouse must receive a notice informing them of their COBRA rights and describing certain provisions of the law (the "Initial Notice") at the time they commence coverage under a group health plan subject to Part 6. Section 606 (a)(4) provides that, upon the occurrence of a qualifying event described in section 603, the plan administrator must give covered employees, spouses and dependent children who are qualified beneficiaries a specific notice of their right to elect COBRA coverage as a result of that event (the "Election Notice"). The type of qualifying event will determine who the qualified beneficiaries are and the required amount of time that a plan must offer continuation coverage to them under COBRA. Pending the issuance of regulations under these COBRA notice provisions, employers and plan administrators are required to operate in good faith compliance with a reasonable interpretation of the statutory provisions. See H.R. Rep. No. 99-453, 99th Congr., 1st Sess. at 563 (Dec. 18, 1985).

You note that in ERISA Technical Release 86-2 (issued June 26, 1986), the Department stated that where the spouse's last known address is the same as the covered employee's, it would consider that an employer or plan administrator has made a good faith effort at compliance with ERISA § 606(a)(1) if the Initial Notice is given through a single mailing by first class mail addressed to both the covered employee and the covered spouse. You ask whether the Department will consider a single mailing addressed to the covered employee, his or her spouse, and dependent children (if any) residing at the same address at the time of the notification to be good faith compliance with the Election Notice requirements of ERISA § 606(a)(4).

It is the Department's position that ERISA § 606(a)(4) gives each qualified beneficiary a separate right to receive a written Election Notice upon the occurrence of a qualifying event permitting him or her to exercise COBRA continuation rights. This requirement may, in some cases, be met by mailing one Election Notice where more than one qualified beneficiary resides at the same address. Where, at the time of the notification, the last known addresses of the covered employee, his or her spouse, and dependent children (if any) are the same, the Department will consider a single first class mailing addressed to the covered employee, his or her spouse, and dependent children (if any) to be good faith compliance with the Election Notice requirements of ERISA § 606(a)(4) in the absence of regulations provided that a separate election notice for each qualified beneficiary is included in the single mailing or, if a single notice is sent, it clearly identifies the qualified beneficiaries covered by the notice and clearly explains the separate and independent right each has to elect COBRA continuation coverage. This letter addresses the factual situation presented in your letter and should not be read as indicating the only way a single mailing may be used to satisfy the Election Notice requirements where more than one qualified beneficiary resides at the same address. See, e.g., ERISA § 606(c).

This letter constitutes an advisory opinion under ERISA Procedure 76-1, 41 Fed. Reg. 36281 (1976). Accordingly, this letter is issued subject to the provisions of that procedure, including section 10 thereof, relating to the effect of advisory opinions.

Sincerely,

John J. Canary
Chief, Division of Coverage, Reporting and Disclosure
Office of Regulations and Interpretations

1 The COBRA amendments added substantially similar provisions to the Internal Revenue Code and the Public Health Service Act. The Internal Revenue Service, the Department of Health and Human Services, and the Department of Labor each has certain regulatory authority in this area. See H.R. Rep. No. 99-453, 99th Congr., 1st Sess. at 562-563 (Dec. 18, 1985). The COBRA provisions in Part 6 generally apply to group health plans covered by Title I of ERISA, but they do not apply to a "group health plan for any calendar year if all employers maintaining such plan normally employed fewer than 20 employees on a typical business day during the preceding calendar year." ERISA § 601(b). COBRA also applies to group health plans sponsored by state and local governments, but those provisions are administered by the U.S. Public Health Service within the Department of Health and Human Services.

Index

About DataMotion Publishing

We Turn Experts into Authors

DataMotion Publishing was originally established to provide books, training materials and other published periodicals to Employment Practices Advisors, Inc. a human resources consulting firm.

Now a full service publishing business, DataMotion provides publishing and related support services to subject matter experts ranging from how-to guides, training materials and practitioners resources focusing on the human resources, legal and general business areas.

Services include:

- Manuscript Services
- Interior Book Design Services
- Cover Design
- Marketing and Promotion Services
- Book Website Development and SEO
- Registration Services

Our team of experts includes not only publishing and related professionals but also experienced writers and experts in the human resources, legal and business arenas.

www.datamotionpublishing.com
info@datamotionpublishing.com

Also by
Diane Pfadenhauer

Workplace Investigations:
Discrimination & Harassment
www.investigateworkplaceharassment.com

The Employer's Guide to New York Employment Laws
www.nyemploymentlawguide.com

The Layoff Book (Coming in 2010)

The Small Business Owners Guide to Human Re-
sources (Coming in 2010)

www.ingramcontent.com/pod-product-compliance
Lightning Source LLC
Chambersburg PA
CBHW021602210326
41599CB00010B/563